ACROSS THE WAY

CHANNELS

John T. Eber Sr.
MANAGING EDITOR

A publication of

Eber & Wein Publishing
Pennsylvania

Across the Way: Channels
Copyright © 2014 by Eber & Wein Publishing as a compilation.

Rights to individual poems reside with the artist themselves. This collection of poetry contains works submitted to the publisher by individual authors who confirm that the work is their original creation. Based upon the author's confirmations and to that of the Publisher's actual knowledge, these poems were written by the listed poets. Eber & Wein, Inc. does not guarantee or assume responsibility for verifying the authorship of each work.

The views expressed within certain poems contained in this anthology do not necessarily reflect the views of the editors or staff of Eber & Wein Publishing.

All rights reserved under the International and Pan-American copyright conventions. No part of this book may be reproduced, stored in a retrieval system, or transmitted in any form, electronic, mechanical, or by other means, without written permission of the publisher. Address all inquires to Rachel Eber, 50 E. High St., New Freedom, PA 17361.

Library of Congress
Cataloging in Publication Data

ISBN 978-1-60880-353-8

Proudly manufactured in the United States of America by

Eber & Wein Publishing
Pennsylvania

A Note from the Editor . . .

It is with warmest regards we meet with you here, at the shore where words of inspiration lap gently without end, beckoning you to depart on a pilgrimage of lyrical composition. Poesy is the universal language of emotions—pains, joys, sorrows, and celebrations—giving voice to any person willing to make an attempt. Composing poetry can be an act of confession and it frees the mind for reflection, new ideas, and beauty. We use verse to announce the important things, to tell our stories, to witness for the record events that matter most: tragedy, loss, frustration but also love, admiration, and the peace of nature. Between these covers, across the pages, people from all walks of life bare their visionary souls for our perusal.

Modern-day poets can face difficulty finding a wide audience, exposure, for their work. Luckily, you have turned the page onto neutral ground for those important expressions, where acceptance can be found among a devoted and passionate community of poetry-enthusiasts: writers and readers alike. To the writers, we hope you treasure your printed work with a sense of accomplishment. It is tangible validation of your stature as a poet. Regardless of skill level, we all can feel the tide of inspiration:

> And I have felt
> A presence that disturbs me with the joy
> Of elevated thoughts; a sense sublime
> Of something far more deeply interfused,
> Whose dwelling is the light of setting suns,
> And the round ocean, and the living air,
> And the blue sky, and in the mind of man,
> A motion and a spirit, that impels
> All thinking things, all objects of all thought,
> And rolls through all things.
>
> —William Wordsworth
> *from* "Lines Written a Few Miles Above Tintern Abbey"

Although Wordsworth speaks of personal memories, we can empathize with his reaction, his swell of sentiments. Sometimes in our lives, we are stirred by feelings so deep, so gut-wrenching—good or bad—that we must tap ourselves with pen and let the excess overflow onto paper.

The beautiful constant of humanity is that we all share in it together; we have individual differences, but our commonalities are far grander in scale. Read the rhymes from your spiritual brothers and sisters and share in their experiences, their suffering and successes. Be wary of impatience, because skipping a single page will mar your poetic odyssey. Be open to serendipity's pen. You can't always predict the effect words will have on you, but ford the distance and you'll be rewarded on the other side with compassion, love, and life vicarious.

Poets great and small all serve the noble task of carrying history forward across time, preserved in print, to inspire and embolden the future. Step confidently into this volume and enjoy the whimsical stories and vivid images as they unfold. We are continually humbled by the talent, honesty, and bravery of our contributors. We thank you, writers and readers alike, for without both there can be no art.

Desiree Halkyer
Editor

A Poem for Sylvia Plath

I recently discovered the purpose and use of
a bell jar, and thought to Myself: "What a waste
of material, and meaning!
But you will always be remembered for the "Bell-jar"!

And what is the purpose of life?
What was the purpose of your life?
Sticking your head in a gas oven, of
odorless, colorless, tasteless death!
Stick a freshly cut orchid flower under a bell-jar,
and hope it doesn't die. And there you have it. A
purpose! Recently I encountered a swarm of bees
and thought, she believed in the Bhagava-gita,
and Krishna's reincarnation. And I go shoo! to a
Queen bee, you bother me.

Wayne Jackson
San Francisco, CA

Pulitzer Prize winner Sylvia Plath was considered one of the greatest poets of the twentieth century. One of the hidden messages of this poem is that her father's occupation during his short-lived life was that of a professional beekeeper.

A Leaf Called Life

A leaf from an ancient tree wends its way to the earth
Traveling on its way floating on a mist called life
It cannot stop, but gently wavers back and forth in the wind
On its way to land at an unknown destination
Sometimes it is a spinning element destined to bloom another day
A breath of life in the earth happy in its place

A leaf can be exquisitely shaped
The air and earth its amiable companion
Its form colored by an artist's pallet and imagination
In its time it can be shaken to the ground by forces unknown
Left to wither and die in a heap of sadness
And then swept away for another time
To live again in beauty to snatch away your heart.

Phyllis M. Anselona
Coral Springs, FL

The inspiration for "A Leaf Called Life" flows from a mind that pauses to view and catch a moment in time. My poems are never planned, but gently and quietly become that written thought. The inner calling and innateness of it all never ceases to amaze me. This particular poem called out softly as an autumn breeze while taking a stroll. The leaves looked so sad and sere as they fell from trees just as life can be at times, but I knew they would blossom again and life would go on and be renewed.

A Dog's Point of View

If I could talk this is what I'd say
I'm glad we were together every single day
You will always be in my heart
because we were best friends right from the start
Please don't be sad
Just remember the good times that we had
the joy and the laughter
and all the toys I went chasing after
I'll be watching you from above
and thank you for giving me a home with lots of love
I really miss seeing your face
together didn't we make this world a better place?
You trained me hard and trained me well
I know I've done my job as far as I can tell
I know what I was meant to do
that was to be there at the right time for you
A part of you is gone
but your life you must continue on
I miss you as much as you miss me
but I guess this was meant to be
I'm in your heart just like you're in mine
I will forever be your faithful canine
We will see each other again
thank you for being my best friend
I can't ease the pain you're going through
just wanted to tell you this from a dog's point of view

Deb Hutchinson
Ligonier, PA

I was so upset when the Pittsburgh Police K-9 dog (Rocco) was killed in the line of duty that I looked at my own dog Rebel and said, "If that happened to you Reb, what would you say?" I wrote this poem in memory of Rocco and to every dog owner in the world.

Across the Way

In Sun-Glow

In my evening,
and your afternoon,
we have found
our time.

As beautiful as Lapis Lazuli is,
or as limitless
as the azure blue sky,
our communion is…

the evening star
at sunset,

an evening prayer
at twilight,

an evening primrose
at midnight,

your kiss at sunrise
in sun-glow,
to me.

Elina Alto
Coconut Creek, FL

The Girl with the Mechanical Arm

Fingers of steel
Jointed elbow
Stitched-in skin
Bolts and springs
To the spinal column
Fused to her shoulder
Deep eyes painted
Lips pursed in ooh
Never falters, never kinks,
Never sputters in woo
Emotions run deep
As she shows
In her mysterious manner
As she keeps in hiding
What she is
From ball to bearing.

Krisann Johnson
Richmond, IN

Across the Way

Williamsburg Project

You see a building standing alone,
I see a place that I called home.
I see my mother calling me.
I see my father hugging me.

You see concrete overgrown,
I see grass and cobblestone.
You see dingy, dirty with grease,
I see curtains blowing in the breeze —
Simple life, if you please.

We ran, we played, all day together
Every day in any weather.
Sun, rain, sleet or snow,
We always had somewhere to go.

They were the projects
And we were *poor*
That was a word that we
Ignored.

Lois Carbo
Farmingdale, NY

Spiritual Whisperings (To a Clairvoyant)

Through a haze I can hear you
at times not very clear
a muffled voice, a cry of pain
a death you cannot bear.
You share with me your life
in both triumph and despair,
we are both seeking answers
though I am here and you there.

A thin line seems to divide us
It's an obstacle we can overcome
for in a clear-open state of mind
we will communicate as one.
If I am granted permission
perhaps a face I'll see,
for this manifested image
is the soul that will forever be.

I pray your restlessness turns to peace
and towards the light I'll look
and what I seek is your release
so I may close your book.

Leonore Canevari
Allentown, PA

I have always had an interest, studied and been involved in a number of successful spirit contacts. Over many years, I volunteered to attempt communication with spirits that were believed to be creating disturbances in both private homes and public businesses. I was inspired to write my poem "Spiritual Whisperings (To a Clairvoyant)" after experiencing some very moving and emotional life stories with spirits that relayed very painful situations surrounding their passing. They were spirits or entities that were experiencing difficulty in their attempt to move on and see the light that would bring them peace.

Across the Way

Quilting Lesson

I thought I saw a butterfly
caressing my daughter's palm.
It was instead her fingers
fluttering
as beneath the willow tree
she stitched poppy petals
with soft embroidery floss
to patches of recycled jeans.

Her needle, wearing crimson threads,
waltzed in and out of one worn denim square
and left behind the portrait of a tiny cardinal.
Through the needle's eye
she swapped red strands
for snowy whites to spread
across the small bird's forest floor.

Quietly, I knelt beside her as she
filled her little pile of worn blue patches
with butterflies and flowers, bees inside
the throats of blooming daylilies,
dragon flies among the cattails,
the best of nature sewn into
a child's quilt.

With its final piece gently stretched across
her open palm, she held down a soft and
pulsing, sunset-shade-of-heart, then signed
beneath it; x x x Mommy

Regina Murray-Brault
Burlington, VT

Winter Solstice

I can remember
A cocoon called December.
Distractions galore —
The plight of the poor.
I will do anything
Just give me more.

More presents and gifts
And spiritual lifts.
Salvation bells singing
Cash registers ringing.
But wait just a moment
My wing-buds are tingling —

Could this be the end
Of a spiraling trend
Down a tunnel of night
Full of unwanted blight?
Or is it — just maybe —
The prelude to light?

Nancy Greenleaf
Portland, ME

Across the Way

Where Shall We Go Today?

"I want to see spring arrive at last,
to watch the buds burst forth and sparrows
splashing in their rainy bath."
I wheeled her out and down the little path.

"I want to feel the summer's breeze, a kiss
upon my cheek so pale.
Feed the ducks along the river bank, walk the
hill and dale."
I wheeled her out and down the same worn trail.

"I want to watch the leaves fall, such glorious
colors to behold. Listen to our stories the
wind in the trees have told."
I wheeled her out and down the little road.

"I want to hold a snowflake, make a snowman,
tall hat and cane, with gloves and scarf, eyes
of coal, singing a winter's refrain."
I wheeled her out and down the quiet lane.

"I want to hear a choir of angels
in that golden ray.
Hold me close, don't cry. Just
stay."
Before I could decide where we'd go this day,
she closed her tired eyes
and slowly slipped away.

Dona D. Welch
Moline, IL

My mother was so smart, so much fun and loved life. We lived miles apart but met each summer to travel exotic places around the world. The minute we returned she would say, "Where are we going next time?" One summer I noticed something very wrong. She was becoming aphasic and soon disappeared into that unknown land of Alzhiemer's. I moved back to care for her. She had forgotten how to talk and walk. As I pushed her in her wheelchair through the seasons, I could hear in my heart what she was saying: "Where shall we go today?"

Purple Sea

Last night I had the strangest dream
One I never had before:
   A dream about a lovely place
Along a peaceful shore.

   The color was deep and beautiful,
Though very strange to me,
   My dream had named this peaceful place
The Endless Purple Sea.

   All fear is gone of what might fall,
When my time comes to pass,
   I feel the calm that I once had,
As a child lying in the grass.

   Back then the clouds made wondrous things
Against the azure sky,
   And they became whatever I drew,
With the pen of my mind's eye.

   I'm not afraid of the endless sea,
As my back grows old and weak,
   For the things I've already had in life,
Are more than what I seek.

   Someday I know I'll walk that shore,
To ask what will come of me,
   And with a happy heart I will take a step,
Into the Endless Purple Sea.

James D. Armbrust
Las Vegas, NV

I don't know how I am inspired to write poetry, so I'll explain with another poem that is just there: As I lie here in my bed, with poems running through my head, I've suddenly come to realize that all the poets I like ... are dead! And that's how I come to write poetry.

Across the Way

My World—Your World

I took a walk the other day
Where as a youth I used to play
I went to see just once again
The fields and streams and wooded glen
And that old sugar maple tree
Stone walls and hidden creature trails
Muskrat borrows along the brook
Wild birds in flight where'er you look
Coon and fox dens here and there
Wild beauty reigned just everywhere
A world it seems made just for me
A place on Earth where I was free

But wait is this the place I seek
It's not a place for hike or trek
Nothing looks the same to me
And where is that old maple tree
There cats and dogs and backyard sheds
Paved streets and cars and flower beds
It's not my private world for play
Too many houses here today
I almost wish I hadn't come
Progress—not for everyone
I sadly turned and walked away
Where as a youth I used to play

Fred T. Mott
Dover, DE

Fred T. Mott, eighty-five years old, lives with his wife Genevive in Dover, DE. They have been married for sixty-two years. They have three married daughters and six grandchildren, all of which live near them. Fred graduated from the University of Georgia and is retired from the US Soil Conservation Service. He is an Army veteran that was assigned to the Air Force. He is the author of a book of poems *Rymes of My Tymes*. His hobbies, besides poetry, include hunting, fishing, decoy carving, and swimming.

Mother's Sadness

She always had the look of sadness on her face
The four children she had could not erase.

Each one had thought the cause was theirs
And often worried in silent despair

Did I cause that pain so clear
In the face that was so dear?

In shameful thought we never asked why
And only through time that passed us by
   Learned the reasons for her sighs.

Her first great love was buried in war
And left the hidden scars so torn
   That shown upon a face we mourn.

Elsie M. Szoo
Galloway, NJ

December 18, 2010

Dear Mom,
I remember when
I was so young
You kindly took me
Under your wing

I was excited and scared
But you calmed my fears
And there were so many
Happy years

You guided me through
So many things
When I had four children
Under my wing

I will always be grateful
As I was from the start
And you will always and forever
Be close in my heart
I love you

Angie Pettigrew
Deland, FL

Dear Mom

I picked you to be my mom
to have you hold me in your arms
and now I feel you slipping away
not loving me in that special way
you're scared and don't know what to do
together we'll make it just me and you.

Don't you want to see me grow
and teach me the things that I need to know
to watch me ride my bike (and)
to watch me hit one into the night
to help me through the good and bad
to dry my eyes when I'm feeling sad.

I need you now more than ever
the one I chose to be with forever
From heaven I came to be with you
if only you will see it through

And when I'm grown with a family of my own
you'll never have to be alone
together we'll watch my children grow
and see the seed that you have sown.

So, Dear Mom, I'd like to say
thank you for choosing me that lonely day
for giving me love and a chance at life
for when it was hard you did what was right.

Robert L. Anselmo
Bethpage, NY

Across the Way

Ode to My Watch

The watch
with a gold band
looks round like as a ring
sitting and shaped in circle form
with a line streak in the middle
it sits solid and very hard
the clock-face and three hands
moving round and round
it never rests
waiting to be worn
to be showed off to many people

All of a sudden
it breaks
rots slowly
the hands work at an abnormal speed
the watch is less popular
the band is wearing down
no one seem to favor it
it is like a ship without a sail

The point of my ode is
vanity is vanity
all is vanity
no matter how good something looks
it's only good for a season

Darian Coleman
Pennsauken, NJ

My name is Darian Coleman. I am a forty-year-old male who comes from a family of eleven children. I was educated in Camden school system and went to college to earn a bachelor of arts degree in sociology from Rowan University. In addition, I earned a master's degree in education from Gratz College in Pennsylvania. I started writing poetry twelve years ago. I prayed and asked God for the gift to write poetry. As a result, I started writing numerous poems throughout the years. Poetry will always be part of my life, and I am anticipating writing a book in the future.

Little Lady of Lace

A springtime sun freckled the table where Joli sat as she sewed.
Sometimes summer rain pebbled the window pane
  as she sewed, sewed, sewed.
Fall found leaves flying on the frosty ground.
  Still she sewed, sewed, sewed.
Sometimes snow pillowed piles of winter white outside the door.
  Still she sewed, sewed, sewed.
At night, lighted candles stroked her fingers
  Her body bent. Her eyes in a squint
  Joli sewed, sewed and sewed.
Slow, steady, close to the white woven before her,
  little lady of lace sewed, sewed, sewed.
Outside, clacking carriages came clattering down
  cobbled streets.
A milky mist rose after the rain and turtle doves
  cooed two by two.
Inside, hooded capes capped pegs along the halls.
  Beneath them all, small wooden shoes sat filled with straw.
An apple sat upon her lap
  breakfast for Joli, not a snack.
  And she sewed, sewed, sewed.
Lace collars for the king.
  She sewed, sewed, sewed.
Lace stockings for the king's court
  She sewed, sewed, sewed.
Lace booties for the royal baby
  She sewed, sewed, sewed.
Her small hands dropped into her lap and quickly
  she caught a noontime nap
  while others sewed, sewed, sewed.

Martha R. Fehl
Brookville, IN

I have always been intrigued with historical facts and fiction. The poem is taken from a completed early chapter book of a loving relationship between father and daughter before the French Revolution. Dickens found an audience for disadvantaged children and I also discovered traces back in genealogy to Louis XIV that piqued my interest. My published credits include 200 different magazines and newspapers in the last fifteen years. With four children of my own, I have been a den Scout leader; A Sunday school teacher, camp instructor, a classroom teacher and substitute teacher.

Across the Way

The Butterfly

A beautiful butterfly lit on the basket of flowers,
As the mourners gathered around the casket.

Its yellow wings fluttered as if listening
To the minister's words of comfort.

She would be buried in this peaceful family cemetery,
Behind the rural church, in
   the shadow of the Blue Ridge.

As the man in the dark suit closed his book,
He committed her body to the earth,
   and her soul to God.

The butterfly must have sensed the grief as it
   flew over the family.
They held tightly to each other in sorrow.

The golden wings hovered a moment
   over the daughter, and then over the husband.
It continued its flight to the site where the
   final resting place would be made ready.

The loss would be felt deeply by those she left behind,
But her soul would find peace with generations of her
   heavenly family.

Judy Sloan
Howell, MI

The Doohickey

While searching around for my wallet
I find this doo-dad in the hall-it
Is a trifle too big
For a thingamajig —
So it must be a watchamacallit!

Dave Rempe
Westerville, OH

Mother Nature's Menu

Oh the sky it is so blue,
The sun is shining oh so bright.
And the glow off the blanket of snow,
Oh how it glows and puts on a show.
The birds are singing pretty songs,
Oh the cardinals so red and so proud,
The woodpeckers with their beautiful
Plumes and red heads, the mourning
Doves with their lovely coos.
This is Mother Nature's menu for today.
Take it or leave it, if you may.
The sparrows say you may not know
What comes tomorrow on these winter days.

Allen Shaffer
Franksville, WI

Across the Way

Ode to My Putter

This putter of mine I'm giving a rest,
    For thirty-plus years it's given its best!
Putts have rolled in from near and far,
    This putter of mine has been the real star!

It's traveled in planes, but mostly by car
    This putter performs wherever we are!
It's been on the courses where the pros hang out
    And courses others might laugh about!

It's hard to imagine what my scores may have been
    Had not this putter kept rolling them in!
For there were many a day when the driver did rest
    And the irons were not at their very best!

The question's been asked.
    Why retire this gem?
I'm not certain what to say,
    Perhaps, it will be in my bag today!

But for now this putter will hang on the wall
    Where friends can view this gem recalled!
"Golf" is the name of the game we play
    The better you score, the better your day!

So, take care of your putter
    And it will take care of you!
You won't make them all,
    But you'll make quite a few!

William P. Bessler
Cincinnati, OH

After retiring from my place of employment where I worked for forty years, I thought about additional changes I might make as I entered this new phase of my life. Since I enjoy the game of golf, I inventoried the equipment in my bag. The only club still with me, after thirty-plus years, was my Lynx putter. I decided it was time to look at the new technology. After many trials and much deliberation, I purchased a new putter. My old reliable Lynx was being retired and it deserved a fond farewell, so I wrote this verse.

Anybody There?

Once I was young and full of life
I had dreams and ambitions to me
The sky was the limit

I had family and friends to pass
The time with, we reminisce about
The good old days over a cup of
Coffee and piece of homemade cake

I enjoyed long walks beneath the
Blue skies, feeling the warm whispering
Breeze blowing upon my face

I welcome the wonders of Mother
Nature the flowers, the birds and
The shade of her green trees

But now that I'm old and seemingly
Forgotten, no one to laugh with or
Tell my fondest memories to

Wisdom I long to share but short
Days and long nights I often find
Myself asking is anybody there?

Barbara A. Kelley
Detroit, MI

I was born Barbara Ann Kelley. I am the mother of seven, a grandmother and a great-grandmother. I started writing poetry in 1989 during my college co-op. I enjoy writing poetry because it expresses beauty in so many ways. I enjoy the invite from my church Antioch MBC when I am asked to write or read one of my poems for a special program or celebration. Poetry writing is a gift to me from a higher power, and I enjoy every chance I get to share the many roads of life.

Across the Way

Storm Warning

He preached that a storm
Was coming someday…
And folks laughed
And folks scoffed
At what he had to say.
But…
That crazy old preacher
Just preached to them more,
And kept on proclaiming
For years of six score.
He built a huge boat
On the brow of a hill,
While people just laughed
And scoffed at him still.
Then something strange happened
That none could explain…
One drop at a time
It started to rain!

Lew Cort
Springfield, MO

Moments

Once in awhile, someone comes along
And touches your heart like a song.

Strangers to friends, we have become,
Enjoying laughter and walks in the sun.

Day to day, moments we share,
Acknowledging how much we care.

Soon time will come when we must part
For new beginnings and brand new hearts.

Life again will never quite be the same
Without you here to play the love game.

Judith DuBose
Orlando, FL

Across the Way

Christmas Eve

Our family's together
This Christmas Eve night.
There's good food and sweets
And everything's right!

Our grandkids are waiting
For old St. Nick.
We have three handsome grandsons
And one cool chick!

There're games to play
And good food to eat.
Then comes the presents,
Oh, what a treat!

The night comes to an end
So home they go,
Tonight Santa comes.
Ho
Ho
Ho.

Susie DeHaven
Logansport, IN

Reflections on a Rainy Afternoon

You are gone...and all the world
seems to have gone with you.
I feel as one dead among the living.
Or am I simply floating in an endless abyss,
unable to grasp...to grasp what?
nothing but *you*—to feel your warmness,
your presence next to me,
and commune, soul to soul.

Marilyn S. Vatter
Oskaloosa, IA

Sanctuary

The snow, stubborn in its all day siege
Came down in dainty little dots
That sparkled as the evening curtain drew
A whitened world, so calm and tranquil
With newly sculpted hills and valleys
A fairyland, yes, but with foreboding

I nestled down in my easy chair
Feet reclined on a needlepoint hassock
Sewn in threads of crimson and blue,
I reached for a cup of spicy cider
Then turned to my book with rapt attention
Deserting the drama that winter had staged

Gertrude Kornfein
Niskayuna, NY

Across the Way

Angels

God so loved us
He sought to guide us
By creating His angels
To be there beside us
To comfort our hearts
In times of sorrow
To always be there
Through all
Our tomorrows

Jeannie C. Smith
North Little Rock, AR

A friend of mine lost a child, and these words came to me. Words sometimes come and I put them to pen so I can remember. And maybe these words and lines will help someone feel better. All in God's time. Peace and love to all in this world of pain and hurting.

Drummer

To hear the beat as I move my feet
The sound is loud and pounds my seat
Sticks are moving
It's a one, two, three beat
When I hit the clash
It brings the heat!
The music is symphony as my cymbals meet
The big bass drum kick
Four on the floor
The one-two roll
That is my soul.
My chest pumping
Sticks spinning in the air
I hear the hum
My top hat high
As I hit the drum!

Kellie Ison
Hilliard, OH

Across the Way

Tomorrow-Dreams

Today,
  it seems,
    has slipped away.

Again, it is tomorrow…

Which with it brings
  more dawning schemes,
  more nightfall sorrow,
More twilight wanderings,
  and a thought
  too ill-defined
    to have a name,
To drift dim-lit gray
  in phantom streams
With flotsam-fraught
  shadows of unwilled
    tomorrow-dreams
That forever wind,
  still the same,
    still on the mind,
Still unfulfilled…

  from yesterday.

James D. Warwick
Houston, TX

The Night Before Christmas in South Vietnam, 1970

'Twas the night before Christmas forty-three years ago
The monsoon erased any thoughts of snow
I wondered what kind of a night it would be
With continuous sounds of artillery
Christmas was coming as I looked at the clock
There was nary a chimney to hang up a sock
Past Christmas memories quickly passed through my head
As I climbed from the bunker and lay down on my bed
Soon the sirens went off and arose such a clatter
We rushed to the ER to see what was the matter
Four incoming wounded were already here
And two KIAs brought up the rear
I looked out the door and gazed up at a star
As the four wounded soldiers went to the OR
They all were drafted and had no choice
But their MDWs gave cause to rejoice
The death and destruction that still lay ahead
Told me I still had plenty to dread
There were no obstacles or coursers to fly
It must have been God way up in the sky
It was now past midnight and Christmas was here
I celebrated by drinking a beer
Once again I lay down on my bed
While visions of mortar rounds danced in my head
I'd think happy thoughts and closed my eyes with a grin
But in just a few hours a new day would begin

David L. Dyer
Grosse Ile, MI

Six years ago at age sixty-eight I developed Parkinson's Disease. That was a calling from God. It had been thirty-seven years since I'd left Vietnam. Knowing I had a story to tell, my brother, Wayne Dyer, internationally renowned author/speaker, often seen on PBS, uttered these words to me: "Do not die with your music still in you." Those words prompted a visit to the Vietnam Memorial, where I traded my alcohol addiction for sobriety in honor of all those names etched on that wall. The lack of alcohol produced insomnia, which in turn put a pen in my hand.

Across the Way

Safe in My Saviour's Arms

Safe in my Saviour's arms,
   I'll bring all my cares and
   lay them at His feet, and I'll rest there,

Safe in my Saviour's arms.
   He'll bear all of your cares,
   Have faith, trust Him, there is nothing to fear
   'cause there's nothing impossible for Him.

Safe in my Saviour's arms.
   He is waiting for you,
   as a parent that cradles His own, safe from all harm,

Safe in my Saviour's arms.
   Safe in His bosom I'll stay,

Safe in my Saviour's arms.

Ruby B. Fleming
Corona, NY

Our Mom's New Home

Mama went home today for she knew the way
He took her in His arms and wiped her tears away
We will miss her and so and we know that quite well
She bade us goodbye from her body so frail
But here with Jesus, she has no more pain.
Rejoice with us, for her new home she has claimed.
In Heaven now, Mama has legs so strong
She is walking and running there around His throne.
Never will she need that wheelchair again
For in her new home, there will be no end.
One day we will join her on the golden shore
And we will praise and rejoice with her forever more.
Thank you, Jesus, for taking Mama home today
And thank you for guiding her all the way.
We haven't lost our Mama, so dear—
Of this we know and have no fear.
For when you lose something you don't know where it is—
But we know where you are, Mama,
For you were and are one of His.
We rejoice with you, Mom.
We will miss you down here!

Iris J. Matthews
Concord, NC

Across the Way

Thoughts of an Evening

Day is done
Gone the sun
From the lakes
From the hills
From the sky
All is well
Safely rest
God is nigh

Fading light
Dims the sight
And a star
Gems the sky
Gleaming bright
From afar
Drawing high
Falls the night

Thanks and praise
For our days
'neath the sun
'neath the stars
'neath the sky
As we go
This we know
God is nigh!

Mary M. Thomas
Breese, IL

Fearfully and Wonderfully Made

Who told you your size is too big or small?
Who told your skin is too dark or light?
Who told you your hair is too kinky or straight?
I hope someone has told you you're fearfully and wonderfully made
God is who said, "You're fearfully and wonderfully made"
Who told you your life would have no future?
Who told you your habit would not be broken?
Who told you your family would always go without?
Who told you your sadness would not someday become joy?
I hope someone has told you you're fearfully and wonderfully made
God is who said, "You're fearfully and wonderfully made"

Barbara J. Collins
Laveen, AZ

My name is Barbara J. Collins the wife of Reverend Loyce Collins. I am a native of Arizona, the youngest of my siblings. I am an alumna of the Fashion Institute of Design and Merchandising and the proud founder of Vessels Ministries. I'm inspired by God and life experiences to write poems. I'm even more inspired when someone can be touched or encouraged by my poetry.

Across the Way

Now and Then

Born on a stormy night
Ready and eager to face my plight
Too soon I faced the real world of blood, sweat and tears
And learned how to cope and calm my fears
I survived the Depression, a wartime marriage and mother of three
I admit there were times when I wanted to flee
At 87, widowed and alone, looking back at what was then,
I wonder: Would I do it all over again?

Bev Levine
Cincinnati, OH

After eighty-seven years of being an only child a devoted daughter, loving World War II war bride, busy housewife, mother of three, grandmother of seven, and great-grandmother of five, here I am, in my too-immaculate, too-quiet apartment. However, I count my blessings, take one day at a time and keep coping.

An Italian Night

Tree shadows seize the park
My heart sinks like the Tuscan sun
Air thick as olive oil and dank
dampens my face and bare arms
cuffed to two beefy bags of groceries

The ricotta moon peppered with pecorino hangs high

Dead leaves the shade of aged Barolo
crunch under my worn black Adidas
adding flavor to the long linguine
dragging
   down the sides
         of each shoe
waiting to be consumed

Hinges grind
   the dark like a knife
      slicing a stale baguette
I shudder at the first bite of a cool crisp gelato
A cork shot *explodes* nearby
Bags slip to the ground
Jars of tomato sauce break

I gag
  S
p i
  n like pizza thrown in the air
I run the other direction
No spaghetti tonight

Keoni Giauque
Federal Way, WA

Across the Way

Don't Listen

I've made some bad choices in my life and for these I feel regret.
But I've done some really good things too and I hope to do more yet.
The past is what it is and it cannot be changed.
I've learned that the sun will still shine bright, even after a cold, hard rain.
Sometimes our paths are chosen for us and we're just along for the ride.
We stagger and stumble and muddle through until we reach our stride.
There are folks who'll try to put you down and make you feel blue.
But just pay no attention to them, because they're not really seeing you.
For they sit so high above us and make judgments on us all.
They like to think they're perfect and that they could never fall.
But they're not as free of sin as they like to think they are.
They believe they're close to Heaven, when they're truly very far.
At least I admit the wrong I've done and will do better with my life.
So I won't let the "perfect" ones cause me any further strife.
I'll continue to do the right thing, I'll give it all my best.
I'll hold tight to all the good in me and let go of all the rest.

Renee M. Tower
Warren, PA

I am a fifty-four-year-old woman, who lives in Warren, PA with my husband, Chuck, and our two dogs, Dugan and Meatloaf! Life isn't always easy and I find writing to be the release I need. It's extremely cathartic and brings me peace, with difficult issues that have been a part of my life. Writing allows me to relate with other people in a way that I could never do face to face. It frees my soul and allows me to say all the things I always wanted to but couldn't.

Spring

The last of winter's flakes have gone
and the ice we used to skate upon.
The sleds with which the children play
have all been stacked and put away.

Nature is being born again
with all the warming sun and rain.
Budding flowers make it clear
that spring has come again this year.

The robin heralds in the spring
with all the different songs she'll sing;
and close against her bright-red breast,
are four blue eggs within her nest.

In country pasture and forest glen
the animal babies are born again;
foals gallop around their mothers in play
and the doe in the forest had twin fawns today.

The little streams sing their own spring song
as over the rocks they babble along.
They're running and jumping so fast
in hopes of catching a river at last.

God gave us four seasons in which to live
for which our thanks we all should give,
but sometimes I find myself wondering
if He didn't put something extra in spring!

Elizabeth A. Greenwood
Columbus, OH

Across the Way

The Policeman

When I go to town as excited as can be
I see a policeman making motion to me.
He is all dressed up and wears a broad smile.
When he blows his whistle, you can hear it a mile.
I start to run but he tells me to stop,
And says "Don't be afraid, I'm a friendly cop."
Then he blows his whistle as loud as he can,
And the first thing you know he's arrested a man;
Who ran a red light and knocked down a child,
And then started off at about 90 a mile.
The police man called the patrol and put the man in
And said, "So long, little girl, I'll be seeing you again."
Now when I go to town I feel safe as can be,
Because the town policemen are looking out for me.

Julia M. Dixon
Hermitage, TN

Afraid

Afraid to live
All taking, never to give
Afraid to laugh out loud
Happiness not allowed
Afraid to dream
Took away my self-esteem
Afraid to think
Thoughts extinct
Afraid to sing
No more meaning
Afraid to love
Push and shove
Afraid to speak my mind
Belittled by mankind

The world made of stone
Makes me afraid and alone
Not a tear I will cry
For I am not afraid to die

Tina J. Clifford
Lewisburg, TN

Across the Way

So Obama Beat Osama, Sir

Barack Obama went looking for Al-Qaeda.
He wasn't in a cave, nor was he in the grave.
Obama went looking for their leader.
He found him in the rear.
His eyes were full of wonder,
His eyes were full of fear.

Shouts rang out in the middle of the night.
It was Obama in a fire-fight.
Chief found Osama still in bed;
And when he rolled him over
He found Bin-Laden dead.

Since he died in a combat zone,
They boxed him up and sank him like a stone,
Destination unknown.

The moral of this tale, you see —
Is not once or twice in Obama's story,
His path of duty was the way to glory.

So Obama beat Osama
And with this measured grief
Tears are changed to joy, back home,
A sweet relief.

So Obama beat Osama
Well how we now know
That's how Barrack Obama
Beat Osama, sir.

Jeffrey Cameron
Green Bay, WI

Channels

Forgetful Me

I guess I'm losing all my marbles
I'm forgetful half the time
Don't remember where I put my glasses
And my cane I cannot find.
Sometimes I open the refrigerator door
Then stand and wonder what I'm looking for.
Went out one day without my teeth
It's getting bad when a person can't eat.
Pleath ith there thum plathe where I can get help?
I don't need to be out of the houthe
Without a leathe.

Guyola Carr
Conroe, TX

I am ninety-five years old, still in good health and staying busy. Sometimes I hear something said and I put a few words together for a poem. I have several — some sad, some funny, some otherwise — all true. Not only do I write poems, I do several crafts: jewelry of buttons and beads, plastic canvas, painting, and more.

Across the Way

Memories, Glad and Sad

First memory began at five,
When my Mom was not alive,
She was called quickly, from above,
And left us, with all our love.
A world war started to shake my nerve,
And my two brothers went to serve,
It came to become a happy day,
When they arrived home to stay.
My sister married and I was alone,
But she and her husband lived close to home.
A few years later I was the bride,
Entered the church, with Dad at my side.
My husband was great and I was glad,
Until God called him and I was sad.
But I had two sons, who were the best,
Who made me happier than all the rest.
I worked for years to help the boys,
And I loved my job, filled with joys.
Now I'm retired and feel so glad,
I have a great life and now, not sad.

Helen L. Bryla
Edison, NJ

Moon Milk and Willow Wine

Any time you're going east
Stop and join us for a feast.
We'll have moon milk and willow wine
And luscious nectars when we dine
Seated at our toadstool table,
Close beside our sea-horse stable.
Maybe you'd prefer rose water
From our little fairy larder.
Dessert will be a baked sunbeam
Topped with a cloud of sweet whipped cream
We'll invite our cricket friends,
And sing with them as daylight ends.
Then we'll settle down to sleep
On fluffy feathers in a heap,
On pillows of smooth silky weaves
Covered with soft maple leaves.

We'll wake when sunrise lights the sky,
You'll take your leave and say goodbye.
We hope you'll come another day,
And maybe you will come to stay
And join our little fairy band
In our peaceful fairy land.

Leila M. Reece
Livonia, MI

Across the Way

To Remember You

America—you are the mother
of freedom and the liberty
for all of us, who comes to you
from many places of the world.

You welcomed them all with open arms—
and gave them the opportunities of a better
life they never had, and asked them to obey
the law of our land—with respect when you
say I do, to become a citizen of America.

Love her—for all she done for you—
that no harm comes to you
if you obey the law—you promised to do—
to become an American.

Otto Valnoha
Fox Lake, IL

Niagara the Falls

Niagara what a wonder,
Niagara what a sight.
Where people go to ponder,
And take a walk in the starlight.
Niagara is beautiful during the day,
Niagara is wonderful at night.
People come from all over wanting to stay,
Not thinking whether it's wrong or right.
Niagara in all its seasons,
Niagara's winter, summer and fall.
Like people and life with their reasons,
As heaven and hell make their call.
Niagara's current runs wild and bold,
Niagara's whirlpool deep as the well.
People have died, stories are told,
And there has been tightrope walkers, do tell.
Niagara with its rainbows and caves,
Niagara is one of seven world sights,
People come to the falls in waves,
With memories and wishes that are bright.

Luis R. Santiago Jr.
Niagara Falls, NY

Poetry in Motion

Poetry in motion
Is so special to see
Between two people
In love

Watching the stars
Twinkling in the eyes,
Of the one that
You love

Dreaming of the way
We met,
Poetry in motion
Is so special
Between two

Watching the stars
Twinkling in your eyes
Makes me so happy
That we are
And always will be
As one.

Sharon A. Birmingham
Glen Burnie, MD

Watch the Morning Come

My brain awakes,
But not my eyes,
They're not ready yet to open,
Not wanting yet to face the day.

But day will come,
There is no doubt,
So brain and eyes you have no choice,
Get up and watch the morning come.

Will it be dark and cloudy?
Or brilliant with the rising sun,
We'll just have to wait and see,
As we watch the morning come.

For many, many, working years,
There was never, ever any time,
To sit and wait,
And watch the morning come.

But now I'm old,
With lots of time,
To sit and wait,
And watch the morning come.

This is the day the Lord has made,
I will rejoice and be glad,
As I sit and wait one more time,
To watch the morning come.

Fern R. Anderson
Niota, TN

Across the Way

War in the Trenches

War in the trenches is a dangerous game.
It drives me crazy it drives me insane.

I stand in the presence of Death and Decay
but this is war, it's just that way.

As we hear the screaming of our friends and the explosion of the
    shells
we all know this is a living hell.

I feel this stuff stuck to my face; is it pasty mud
or mucky blood.

The action is so loud no one hears me screaming or crying
because most of my friends, they are dying.

We keep on fighting because we are strong
singing and marching along.

War in the trenches is a dangerous game.
As long as there are battles the soldiers will remain.

Jordon L. McCready
Crisfield, MD

Dad

The snow fell slowly by the window
At dawn the frozen air
Crept through the house
And took his soul away

Back to where it started
In the fields, the meadows
Down by the pond in the woods
Through the wind to the sunlight forever

Scott Moyer
Duncansville, PA

A Birthday Poem to All Cat Lovers from One Grateful Cat

If I could speak with you, this is what I'd say:
Thank you for kindness and loving care each day.
You never fail to seek me out and fill my every need,
you never have a "favorite"—a female, male or breed.
And when I'm hungry, you always fill my dish,
it's just as if you seem to know my every whim and wish.
I really don't know how you do it, but the talk going 'round us now
is that we're so glad you love us, you really are the
    "Cat's meow!"
And so with all my feline friends and many meows and cheers,
we wish you *"Happy Birthday"* followed by many happy, healthy years!

Frances Vickers
Malverne, NY

Summer

Cool summer,
A shady hillside and green grass high
Quiet summer,
A gentle breeze and a soft blue sky
Long summer,
A daydream and a bee buzzing by
Short summer,
A light rain and leaves that die.

Tom Flickinger
Washington, PA

I was a freshman in college when I wrote the poem to my high school sweetheart. Her favorite season was summer and I wanted my poem to remind her of summer. We have spent many summers together as we approach thirty-eight years together as man and wife. It has been a love filled with summer thoughts.

Channels

Step It Up!

Don't fret,
We're not home yet, step it up
While it's day
Let the Lord have His way, step it up,
God didn't raise no dummy and Jesus was no mummy.
So step it up! Step it up! Step it up!
Don't abort, life is too short.
Step it up! Step it up!
Time waits on no man.
Do what you can and step it up, step it up!
Are you a roller or a stroller?
Step it up, step it up.
Am no liar or a vampire.
Step up your plan.
It's in the hand of the man
So why don't you step it up, step it up?
Go around and you might miss town!
Step it up, step it up!
Eat at the table.
It will make you stable.
Step it up, oh step it up!
Finally, Jesus bled to raise the dead.
Why don't you step it up, step it up,
step it up, step it up?!

Joseph Mercer
Garysburg, NC

My name is Joseph Mercer. My poem, "Step It Up!" Is based purely on my personal experiences in life. I am the oldest of five siblings, three boys and two girls. I felt that my poetry work was divinely inspired by our creator God. I am a born-again Christian who loves the Lord. I was born and raised in a loving home by good parents who led me in their footsteps of faithfully attending church. Our hometown is Elizabeth City in North Carolina. I am so proud to be a participant in leaving my mark in the world with so many of you who share the same interests as I do on impacting the world in a positive way. Thank you very much fellow lovers of poetry.

Across the Way

God Can Wait

I cannot give up
I cannot give up
I could not make my dreams come true
No matter how many assemblies, bullying will go on
But not in Heaven
In Heaven I can do what I want
They don't understand
Taking a pill in the morning—every morning.
I can't—not now
If I'm going to get bullied, I can't give up
Bullying is part of life
I've tried giving up—I can't
I would be missed…..but I can't
I shouldn't, but I need to…..but I can't
Washington didn't give up on the Delaware,
Martin Luther King, Jr. didn't give up
I can't
God can wait

Peter Delaney
Princeton, NJ

When We Weren't

A long time ago,
I wonder how things were,
All us humans,
Were erased from the earth's soil.

A dinosaur must have laid his feet,
Just where I am standing,
And where a large synagogue was erected,
A four-toed lizard must have scurried through the sand.

Currently,
New York City is its own bubble,
With buildings springing out from the ground,
Every street corner I turn.

In the days of the dinosaurs,
Only animals set foot on the rough terrain,
Battling for the limited resources on the land,
But enjoying the landscape,
Freed from various architectural works.

Evolution is its own little game,
Each city expanding its bubble,
Increasing its capacity for progress,
But keeping its distance from perfection.

Zaul Tavangar
New York, NY

Across the Way

A Late October Dusk

Give in to the golden filter
And let its beauty tint
Your vision, let it hinder
The very way you think.

Give pigment your permission
To alter what is real,
Diminishing division
'Tween truth and what you feel.

Let the hue consume
The grander universe,
Creating the sweetest view:
A late October dusk.

Clare Ellen Corbett
Bronx, NY

Ode to My Dog

On winter mornings
she lays beside my
bed.
When I walk up
and down the
halls she is
there with me.
When she is barking
it is my job to feed her.
I love my dog.

Turner Wells Hamilton
Princeton, NJ

My Time

My time on Earth is over,
and I know I'm going home
to be with Jesus and my friends,
so you know I am not alone.
The angels came and took me
to see the Crystal Sea.
How glorious to see my Lord;
He means everything to me.
Please do not cry for me
For I am in Heaven and finally pain free.

Carol Burkhart
Wooster, OH

Majesty of the Sea

(Petrarchan Sonnet Form)

She keeps her secrets hidden deep and dark,
Mysterious in her fathoms unknown.
The poor damned souls of sailors she has thrown
To the dead eyes and white teeth of the shark.
In a storm of rage she shall take back the spark
Of life, given to men but in a loan.
Drowning always in waters cold as stone,
Are the sunken bones of ships, bleached stark.

Yet in her great temper is majesty,
And a challenge issued to those of men
Brave enough to embark upon her waves.
Like a bird who longs to be wholly free,
So their hearts long to set sail once again.
It is the beautiful sea their soul craves.

Leah A. Duff
Exton, PA

Live Another Day

Standing in the sun, after all of the rain has gone
Standing where the soft wind blows, it's all you've ever known
Nothing seems to matter when we stand so far away
From every problem we might ever have, it's just another day

Go to sleep and dream it off, those things that haunt your wake
Tell them that they can't hurt you, and your soul, they can't take
Someday we will leave this place, and head so far away
Someday we will leave this place, and live another day

Patience is a virtue, but that day is drawing near
No longer waiting in the shadows, gone is all your fear
He's coming forth to bring us home, it's not that far away
He is coming for us all, so we can live another day

Just another day, live another day
Someday we will leave this place, to live another day
Stow away your problems in the pockets of tomorrow
And come join us in that journey
We will live another day

Whitney B. Bevins
Gate City, VA

Across the Way

Laughter

Bellowed or hollowed
A giggle or a chuckle,
Will it just be a small laugh
Or one that will make your knees buckle?

For a laugh is a simple gift
Granted to us each day,
An invitation handed on a silver platter
Inviting us to partake.

A hoot or a snort,
Nonpareil is this gift
It never encumbers,
And it releases all lenitives.

You don't have to be sentient
A laugh is simply not a crime,
Laughing is an orotund
A memory that's worth your time.

Will it echo or fade
Sink and die down?
None of those things
Because, my child, a laugh simply turns your day around.

Ashwini Selvakumaran
Dobbs Ferry, NY

Poetry has always been my passion. I eat, sleep, and breathe words. Having a father who is a diplomat, my family always ends up moving to different places. We have been to places far, far away like Yemen and "home-base" like Canada. I can always make new friends, but poetry is a way for me to express my inner emotions—my feelings and thoughts. Poetry is how I express and answer the question, who is Ashwini Selvakumaran?

The Spirit of Jezebel

The spirit of Jezebel can cause you great harm,
Stay far from her and all of her charm.
She is a woman of ungodly intentions,
Who will destroy anyone who comes close to her dimensions.
This type of person has no scruples,
And she will use any one of her pupils.
She is found in churches, school, home and work,
For she especially shows up those places to lurk.
She causes major division, confusion and strife,
For she brings utter devastation into your life.
If you permit her to come she will never leave,
She will just keep smiling to make you believe.
She's as evil as anyone can be,
Test her spirit and you will see.
She's controlling and only concerned for her own well being,
She will never admit to your way of seeing.
Seeing your side to any of your aspect,
For she doesn't care for she has no respect.
She never listens to anyone in authority,
For it's only how she sees her own priority.
Who she can take down with her to the pit,
For she is skilled with amazing wit.
This kind of spirit only bears bad fruit,
For she came from the worst of the devil's root.
She's charming, convincing and very sweet,
Buy into her charms that will be your defeat.

Gail A. Alexander
Pembroke Pines, FL

I am a wife of a loving and caring husband of thirty-six years, and a mother of three daughters. I am also a grandmother of two granddaughters, both of whom turn four years old this year. My love for writing poetry came at an early age in junior high school. My teacher told me I had a promising future to become a great writer someday. This poem was inspired by doing a study of the Jezebel spirit in the holy Bible. My hope is to inspire others with strength, wisdom, and knowledge in knowing the Lord.

Across the Way

Strength of His Hand

The strength of my Lord's almighty hand
encouraging and helping me to stand.
My hope is in the strength of His hand.

Healing my body again and again.
Upon my Savior I can depend.
My healing is in the strength of His hand.

Directing and guiding, my teacher is He.
A disciple like Him, I want to be.
My purpose is in the strength of His hand.

Jesus gave His all with His great love.
Sent down to me from my Father above.
My love is in the strength of His hand.

Giving me comfort. Lifting me every day.
In His presence I want to stay.
My peace is in the strength of His hand.

My faith is growing with keeping Him near.
Abating discouragement. Abating the fear.
My faith is in the strength of His hand.

His blessings surprise me. My cup He does fill.
Meeting my needs at His good will.
My blessings are in the strength of His hand.

Salvation is the gift He freely gave.
For all the world He came to save.
My salvation is in the strength of His hand.

Bonnie F. Tucker
Clarksburg, WV

When

Dreamed of the day *when*,
  but it never seemed possible.
I searched and I searched to find *when*,
  again it slipped through.

Waiting my days
  and crying my nights.

Found a *when*
  Thought it was secure
But to my surprise
  the *when* fooled me.

Waiting my days,
  and crying my nights.

Open a little more
  I said, inside my hearts depth
Fooled again of that *when*.

Waiting my days
  crying my nights.

I no longer dream of *when*.
For she had betrayed me true
and I would rather not
dream of it again.

Waiting no days
  but crying my nights.

Nancy E. Abernathy
New London, NC

Across the Way

Angel of Death

She crouched atop the rocky cliff,
And stared into the deep abyss.
Her wings were clutched against her back,
As her mood fell to black.
Her wings were like the darkest night,
And her features ghoulish white.
She is what nightmares revolve,
For she is the darkest of angels.
However deep inside the fright,
Lay hidden a heart and soul that yearned to shine bright.
She wanted to give up the dark,
But she knew it had left its mark.
The evil had left her wings tainted,
A black that could never be painted.
The white angels looked at her with disgust,
And she knew she would never fully gain their trust.
Now she sits and dreams of a future day,
A day the black will dissipate.
Then her light will shine so bright,
It will even shine through the darkest of nights.

Tiffany Hoard
Coeur D'Alene, ID

Life Goes On for the Unknown

We have this good thing
I made my choice by giving you that ring.
Our children came and we are growing
our fear for them by not knowing.
As time passes we gracefully last
and seek fortune and peace among the masses.
Our health fails us when our strength compels us
to continue seeking the unknown.
We think our plans are sure because we plan to endure
only to find lurking the unsure.
Why must we continue this strategy when life's ending is unknown?
I go back to the beginning not caring for the ending
having hope in this unknown thing by giving you that ring.

Jerome E. Walker
Los Angeles, CA

Across the Way

No Turning Back

When in this life, all pain is gone,
no looking back from whence we roam.
If we could see what lies ahead,
Would we complain as once we did?

I do not know, but probably so,
for so you see, our eye can't see
those lights ahead, or Gates of Pearle
that open wide, but even then,
we must go on.

As we go on, we're almost there,
The lights grow brighter, and ahead we see
a Gate of Pearle, and now we know
We've won the race, all because we kept the pace.

Such love and peace cannot compare,
For now we know we won the race,
We stood the test, we did our best,
For we have reached
Our heavenly home.

Betty M. Moore
Seneca, SC

In memory of my husband Harold D. Moore, my parents Joseph Frank and Carrie Collins Morgan, and my dear brother the Rev. Frank Douglas Morgan. My life is a canvas of who I am, may that canvas reflect that Christ lives within and He can still do the same today as when He walked the shores of Galilee.

The Ranch

They all raised me, made me who I am, the better me,
my grandfather, my grandmother, the Ranch.
My grandparents looked like grandparents were supposed to look,
but the Ranch was paradise.

A paradise surrounded by a burning, scorching hell populated by
Angels disguised as trees too tall for me to see the tops of,
Cottontails who mowed the lawns at night,
their eyes lit like stars when they looked toward me at twilight,
Mesquite mazes for a playhouse wait to be built by my imagination
And a pool so cold from artesian flow, I was baptized anew with
    each plunge.

Papa is dead. Nana is in a nursing home.
The Ranch, structures, trees, pyracanthas, all to be bulldozed in a
    week.
No homeless will trespass according to my father.
He has the money now, but will let nothing of charity remain.

I dig up a rose bush gone wild.
I search for one last arrowhead,
one shard of broken china once in Nana's kitchen,
still buried in the trash heap on the far side of the levy.
I etch my mind with all the images I can while there is still light.
I leave through the gate, on a dirt road I walked daily to and from
    school.

Later my life in shambles, I want to hurt myself more than I can
    bear.
I want to die. I will. I drive toward the Ranch.
I will see it gone, destroyed, the worst hell I can imagine.
I'm a mile away. I stop. I can't confirm that it is gone.

Linda Viviane Lester
Reno, NV

Across the Way

Frozen in Time

My heart's on fire
My mind's frozen in ice
Which path do I choose
To create a good life?

My gut is true
My soul is gold
Yet why all of these stories
And lies you told?

Loyal and unselfish
Honest and smart
Why can't my heart
Just melt my mind apart?

Soul of gold
Gut of truth
It's like a blessing
With a sprinkle of youth

Ice and fire and rocks
Thrown at me through life
Now buckets surround me
Fire melting my ice like a knife

The use of a candle flame
To thaw my mind
That's when your heart and
Mind become one and combine

Cassandra Faustino
Peabody, MA

Mother Dear

How the years pass so,
I find myself loving you for
All the things you sow.
You've given of yourself and rarely
say "I love you so," but your
actions speak so loud that
the love is so aglow.
As a young widow perhaps the
years for us growing up were
difficult for you, but we learned
a lot about love from you because
you shown us anew.
And if we disappointed you
somehow along the way, we still
have the love to share that you
have given us each day. I thank you
   for being our mother
and bringing the love, the love that
will unite us with the love above.

Elizabeth Mylod
Oradell, NJ

The Knowledge of Me

Of people, of places
Of love of men
Once I discovered
Did my life begin

Of planes, of trains
Of automobiles
Deep valleys, vast lands
Great tall hills

Of life, of love
Of sadness and pain
Joy and death
Loss and gain

Of God's love
Of God's favor
Satan's tricks
Disguised with flavor

Of a feel
Of a touch
So human
So much

Of these things
I feel and see
Comes the knowledge and experience
Of being Me

Laura P. Smith
Pinebluff, NC

Consequences

Oh consequences
It's true
That nothing else can
Convince us
Of anything as you
So constantly do.
We tend to deny
That you will justly appear
By simply being a mirror.
We often gladly pray
You'll gently fade away
As night does before each day.
Yet, it is completely clear,
While in a very precarious way
You are here for the duration
With an equal smile on our
Due diligence
And extended vacation.

Jae Lee
Lakeport, CA

While pondering the connections between words, actions and inertia, and recognizing the inevitability of the one thing leading to another, the beginning of my poem "Consequences" came to mind. I was inspired to develop it; whether working or playing, the results of our choices may be subtle, haunting, daunting, or sublime. I live in a friendly community near a majestic lake in Northern California. I teach Dr. Bates Method for improving eyesight and I am a certified massage therapist. I enjoy my affinity to poetry, photography, organic gardening, reading, writing, hiking, and traveling, especially to visit my two adult sons.

Across the Way

I Want More of This Bread Now

I do not want more rye
or white
or whole wheat
or potato
or challah
or raisin
or Italian
or French
or multi grain
or oatmeal
or zucchini
or pumpernickel
or date and nut
or focaccia
or pannini
or sour dough
or semolina
or baguette
What I want some more of
is "bread" as in money *now*

Augusta Abramczyk
Woodhaven, NY

The Tall Oak Tree

Oh let me sit by the side of
the road
Beneath the tall oak tree
where the shadows fall and
the cool breeze flows
under that tall oak tree
Abraham sat 'neath a tall oak tree
And the Lord come to visit
him there,
Oh what a glorious time they
must have had visiting and
eating there
As I sit here 'neath the tall
oak tree
I know He visits me here
For I hear in the wind a
sweet gentle voice
And I feel His presence near

Martha M. Boring
Johnstown, PA

When I read the Bible or other books in my mind, I can place myself with characters and the place where they are at the time. It's a wonderful thing.

Across the Way

Purpose

God created each one of us for a purpose; pray and believe in Him each day
Trust in the Lord to uphold you, and to guide you along the way
The devil is here to tempt you; he comes to fill you with doubt and fear
But insist on fulfilling your purpose; the Lord God is always near.
God created each one of us for a purpose, as He created Heaven and Earth
Surely, He knew about our existence before our mothers gave us birth
God is our Heavenly Father; stand faithfully in His name
Listen obediently to His words, and you will never be the same.
Never give up or fear; courageously go through the fire
Fulfilling your purpose for the Lord is your greatest desire.
Never look back in dismay; positively fight for victory.
Someday your purpose will be accomplished; someday the Lord will say
"Well done" to thee.

Deonette Berry
Brooklyn, NY

My name is Deonette Berry. Writing poetry has been a hobby of mine for approximately thirty years, sometimes a way of expressing my feelings without speaking to another person. My goal is to uplift the spirit of others, in what I say and what I write. So, I encourage them to 1) one never give up, even when they encounter times of failure, and 2) rebuke all doubts and fear, when they tend to draw near. It makes me happy when someone tells me that the words of one of my poems has had a positive effect on their life.

Memories

Roses bloom only for a short season
For everything on Earth there is a reason
If we open our hearts and just look around
At all the roads we chose to travel down

When we come to our golden years
We will have had sorrow laughter and tears
If we have stopped to help someone along the way
There will be peace in our soul at the end of the day

We need to see the beauty as each day begins
For life is a journey from beginning to end
When our memories take us to a place in the past
We will find the love in our hearts is all that lasts

Betty J. Russell
Cleveland, TN

Across the Way

Sleep Baby Sleep

My little one so precious and small, innocent and sweet, the most beautiful of all.
Nighttime has come, and it's time for bed, as the stars twinkle brightly over your head.
Close your sleepy eyes, and rest your little head, snuggle up in your fluffy blanket, in your own little bed.
  Sleep baby sleep.
I'll read you a story to help you to sleep, and I pray that in God's hands you He will keep.
I hope your dreams are of wonderful things, of all the joys that each new day will bring.
Out the window sits the moon in the sky so low, big and round giving off a soft, yellow glow.
  Sleep baby sleep.
I hope you grow up to be happy and strong, and learn in your heart what is right and what is wrong.
Sometimes the world can be an unkind place, but in my loving arms you will always be safe.
The clock on the wall is beginning to chime, the hour is late precious child of mine.
  Sleep baby sleep.
Nighttime is a quiet time, everything is so still, except for that little cricket singing in the windowsill.
Look whose sleeping, curled up on the rug, purring ever so softly, your little kitten, my love.
Even the birds are quiet now, listen, you don't hear a thing… until the sun comes out again and they begin to sing,
  Sleep baby sleep.

Gail M. Tucker
Albuquerque, NM

Channels

Surrendering

Under the blazing suns,   moon-dark nights,
fogs
musical rains,   resting,   swishing-tail quiet.
Oh how I yearn to soothe their sweet heads with
steady hand.
One day I will walk out there.   I will.
Instead
I stare at you amazed.   In the morning air
your sounds singing to me again
when it's feeding time.   Each day
your light filled my sky. Never alone in the garden was I.
Their angus faces steeped in dark,   deep listening and
heads down.
Lulled into thinking they would be there
forever.
Change   Desire this   Savor that
They have asked so little of me.   How can
I take it back now?
Our air   dense — wet with sadness.

I had a dream last night that
I stroked their sweet heads with
steady hand.

I never knew
how fragile   they were.

The farm was put on the market today.

Gail Huntley
Hancock, NH

Across the Way

My Dog Missy

I had a dog who was not only my pet, not a friend, but
  was more like a child.
When she used to get happy, and wanted to play she would
  go wild.
Missy was her name.
No other dog will ever be the same.
She was affectionate and loving when she was with me.
A dog or any pet becomes part of a family.
She was always playful right from the start.
She turned out to be so smart.
She became part of my life when she was eight weeks old.
It's never easy to have a puppy do what they're told.
She saw me grow up from when I was thirteen.
In all of her thirteen years she was never mean.
I'd hide from her and she'd look for me.
Then she'd find me and bark happily.
She loved playing with the ball and would take it away.
She was fun to play with every day.
I'd ask her to give me a hug, then a kiss.
That's one thing about her that I'll always miss.
She had a way of showing that she loved me.
Oh what a wonderful dog was she.
If she did something bad, she knew I'd get mad.
But no matter what, throughout all the years, she
  was the best dog that I ever had.

Drusila Rodriguez
New York, NY

Our Choices…

We didn't choose our natural parents, nor do they ultimately choose what we will be,
We came here with varying gifts and talents for the world to experience or see.

We each decide whether we will speak or quiet our voice.
It is we alone, who finally make our choice,

We are all given individual opportunities to use or to waste,
Though at times we find ourselves reacting in haste.

Yet who knows which of us will have a solution, healing or cure,
For a world in need of prosperity to secure,
If we would but the criticisms endure.

We learn many things during our journeys here,
Some life changing, others to discard,
Selfishness at times masquerades as fear,
And has its own reward.

But to not go boldly is to lose, if we so choose.

Although at times we attempt to be aloof,
The pursuit of acceptance often encourages the denial of truth.

Ted Brown
Las Cruces, NM

Societies have existed and will exist to advantage some and disadvantage others. We are all sent to Earth by our Creator to learn, live, share, and receive, but above all else, to be blessings, both to ourselves and all others. Forgiveness is a powerful ointment; use it freely. Enjoy your Earth journey, you are designed to do just that!

Across the Way

Elizabeth

The complex journey of life
  begins the day we are born

Childhood
  a carefree stepping stone
    before we are thrust into adolescence

The remainder
  an uphill climb
    with steep mountains, deep valleys,
      rolling hills, rushing waters, pristine forests

Elizabeth
  lost part of her childhood
    stripped away
      by the unforeseen deaths of her mom and dad

Struggling
  to rise above the forbidden grief,
    she put one foot in front of the other
      and continued on the difficult journey

A loving mother
  taking good care of her children
    trying to rise above that heavy, unbearable burden of her childhood

Pain
  all around her, yet persevering like a sun that never really sets

May the heavy weight lighten
  as Elizabeth is lifted up in God's loving hands

May her pain cease

Margie Gary
Vancouver, WA

The Wretched Old Man

A man I know he schemes and plots,
He holds his wife in chains.
He rules the roost, he calls the shots,
"'Cause women got no brains!"

He tells her when, he tells her how,
His voice so strict and stern.
With brazen voice and risen brow,
His orders harsh with burn.

He struts with pride, "I have the say!"
A sentence often spoke.
Then curses loudly, black and gray,
So brashy you could choke.

The day had come when she was not,
Not known was death or flee.
This wretched man was in a spot,
Yet blamed her endlessly.

His life's end near, still one more punch,
"Where's family and my friends?
Their help I need, that useless bunch!"
Again, as he offends.

His dying breath, still cross and mean,
No person there to hear,
Was laid to rest, no mourners seen,
Not one to shed a tear.

Pamela K. Furstenberg
Illiopolis, IL

Across the Way

When Bugles Blew

Hail to you our heroes
Who fought in Vietnam
And lay aside the lie, my lads
That we didn't give a damn
When bugles blew the call went out
Across our country wide
Over hills and dales and meadows
And down the mountain side
You did not wait nor hesitate
You did not ask what for
You only heard the bugles blow
Our country's call to war
A war like no other war
With battle lines arrayed
But orange mist and boobie traps
And Charlies fire and fade
Vietnam oh Vietnam
Whose sanguine face was seen
Live in living color
On our nightly TV screen
Yes you are our heroes
Heroes beyond par
And when you heard the bugles blow
You did not ask what for

Charles F. Burkhalter
Baytown, TX

Alphabet

A is for Amy it's also for apple.
B is for the brook and sounds like a babble.
C is for country, it's also for city.
D is for daisies for they are so pretty.
E is for elephant with his big long nose.
F is for feet with ten little toes.
G is for girls, it's also for go.
H is for happiness that we all should know.
I is for ice cream that I get in a cone.
J is for jump rope it's also for Joan.
K is for kittens who like to purr.
L is for lamb with his curly fur.
M is for mother and also for me.
N is for the nuts squirrels hide in a tree.
O is for onions that burn your eyes.
P is for playmate but also for pies.
Q is for quail, they are little wild birds.
R is for rhinoceros that travel in herds.
S is for school, where we learn to read.
T is for teachers that we really need.
U is for unicorn with a horn on his head.
V is for vitamins we take before bed.
W is for wolf that we leave alone.
X is for x-ray that shows us a bone.
Y is for yesterday, wasn't it fun?
Z is for zebra, he likes to run.

Alex Sorrell
Las Cruces, NM

Across the Way

Same Mistakes

Drugs exacted their cruel measure
Her belongings, devoid of any treasure
A set of works was all she had
Her existence gone — it was so sad
Her short life over at twenty-one
A teenager destined for fullness and fun
She knew it all and came to the City
But it swallowed her up — what a pity

A new arrival like spring's first bloom
Devoured by pimps to a life of gloom
Johns, drugs and cigs were her daily feed
A vacuous life — always in need
An overdose claimed her, no one will mourn
A crumpled street urchin, so forlorn
A cop saw promise amidst all her fear
And turned his head to wipe a tear

She now rests in peace — her life complete
Others will take her place on the street
Life moves on without second takes
Doomed to repeat the same mistakes

Dan J. Kelleher
Ballston Lake, NY

I am a third generation New York City cop. In the 1960s, Times Square was my first assignment. The lure of success and fame beckoned youngsters to the bright lights of Broadway. Street predators found some first and opened doors to drugs and death. I saw this repeated too many times.

Three True Diamonds

This pen reacts through the grace of God.
I twitch and toss and sting and prod.
The answers to which I may never find,
Regarding poor decisions made in an altered state of mind.
Three precious unique nuggets of gold,
Three destined for me to never hold.
Of them I speak, my voice in strain,
To touch and jest but forbidden to contain,
For now with prayer I understand,
They're their own, not mine, spun solely by our Lord's hand.
With this realization I bow to weep,
Now with clarity not mine to keep.
Three true diamonds fashioned from the rough,
Stern and bold, sensitive yet tough.
For they have lived the path of test,
Grit and claw, days void of rest.
My pride unequaled for each of all,
Alas! My voice cannot hail face pressed to wall.
They have wallowed in hell and laid down in heather,
Not of this house yet closer together.
Of Katie, Mitchell and Emma I write,
I, surrounded by darkness, and they are my light.

Gary Findley
Napa, CA

Across the Way

Simple Life

Waking to a beautiful dawn
To watch the sun dance on the water beyond,
The crisp fall air,
The smell of autumn everywhere
A glistening frost
In the shiny mist,
The crunch of leaves beneath my feet.
The deer they rut,
The coyote howl
The hoot I hear among the owls.
The geese, they flock,
The eagles soar.
The river rages;
Then it is no more.
November light cascading
Through leaves of red and gold.
I know winter comes calling,
The North wind soon will blow.
December skies of a gloomy gray
Bring drifts of glistening white.
Easy, no, it will never be,
Yet beauty so abounds,
This simple life is perfect;
It takes my breath away.

Julie Beck
St. Libury, IL

Dancing Girl

There is a dancing girl
with a smile on her face
She looks like a flower could
gently move through the air

  Dancing dancing she goes
imitating the rhythms
from the music that sweet
is playing her song

  Her skirt is waving
Her red blouse is silky
and her hair is shiny
like the brilliant sun

  There is a dancing girl
spinning around so well
Dancing dancing she goes
like the sun and the wind

Javier Atristain
Manteno, IL

Across the Way

Through a Child's Eyes

Kids ask the funniest things especially when you say to them
I am sick, they look at you with expressions of sadness and wonder what can they do to help you get fixed.
  When you tell them you are broken and won't be quite the same, they look at you in amazement and think you must be insane.
  I told my child I had cancer and I might die; I was too harsh… he started to cry.
  I said, I'm sorry, honey, I didn't mean to scare you; God loves me and you and everybody, He will bring me through.
  He said I love you too, Momma, and we looked at each other and smiled; I said thank you, honey, because God knows all, and sees all we just have to wait a little while.
  The day finally came when I didn't have hair on my head or my face; he looked at me and said I love your funny face.
  The expression on his little face it was so cute and funny; I said I know I look different but thank you, honey.
  He asked is God gonna give you back your eyebrows—your eyelashes and your hair? I looked at him and laughed and said, yes He will because He said—He promised, He will always be there.
  Kids are so funny they always say what's on their minds; I said thank You, Lord Jesus, thank You for me, my loved ones, and for all mankind.

Minnie Sims-Aubrey
Magnolia, AR

My inspiration comes from the Holy Spirit. God has brought me through all the chapters in the book of my life. I'm a twenty-five-year breast-cancer survivor with four beautiful children, a new husband and three more beautiful children, and the hope of many more chapters in my continuing book of life. God keeps on keeping me and enabling me to write my life's journey in the form of poetry. I have learned to let go and let God, in the mighty name of our Lord Jesus Christ. Amen.

Walking with Grandpa

Through fields of golden dandelion circles
bending under sunny skies

"Damned weeds," the old man growled.
"No, no," the young voice cried,
"these are flowers for my mommy."
"Now, now," Grandpa whispered,
"Come sit with me, I know a flower secret.
This golden circle beneath your chin,
means you're sweet as butter and love dwells within."

… the season passes…

Through fields of white dandelion balls
swaying under clouds of grey

"Damned weeds," the old man groaned.
"No, no" the young voice called out to say
"these are puffs of magic kisses from my grandma!"
"Now, now," Grandpa once more whispered
"we'll make a necklace for your grandma.
We'll take the stems and weave a chain,
like circles without ending, her love for you remains."

Shirley A. Engelmann
Germantown, WI

Across the Way

Can Any?

Some may ask, can out of Pure Michigan's Benton Harbor come any good a thing
When lots of girls babies are having?
When crime is rampant and children out of school are dropping?
When jobs are going and businesses are closing?
Yes, my heart is hurting!
Many a good thing has come out of Benton Harbor:
My start of a new life as a little girl,
My close-knit family and friends awhirl,
My education in those formative years so empowering,
My husband and my two lovely daughters all a blessing!
Benton Harbor has birthed many a good thing!
Great teachers, doctors, lawyers, nurses, husbands, wives, children;
Relationships that grew and blossomed ending in marriage.
Children were born, mine included, who went on and made success stories.
Actors, comedians, athletes and professionals on the world stage.
There've been several success stories from Benton Harbor.
Though you don't hear a lot about them, doesn't change the fact that they're awesome too.
Sinbad the actor and comedian, Wilson Chandler a pro basketball player are only two.
My children—employees of the US Government helping to protect us—are others.
Safe to say there're some good parents and grandparents out of Benton Harbor.
Pity my husband, after a massive heart attack, couldn't see his daughters graduate from college.
Lester had insisted the girls go away from home to seek knowledge.
Lesha, so attached to Daddy, wanted to stop college at junior year.
Mama, though desperately needing company, encouraged her to stay another year.
Thank God both struggled and graduated with cheer!

Maxine A. Smith
Benton Harbor, MI

I'm Maxine Smith. I was born in Millington, TN in 1960 and moved to Benton Harbor in 1972 with my sister and her husband. I attended Benton Harbor High School and graduated with my diploma in 1979. I was married for twenty years to Arlesta Smith. We had two daughters. We are a close-knit family that believes in prayer. I'm a widow. My niece told me about computer classes. I decided to take the opportunity to be computer literate. The instructor George S. Agoki, PhD really inspired me to write this poetry. Poetry is a way to pour out my heart.

He's Gone for Now

Each night I kneel
  to say my prayers,
I hear your footsteps
  on the stairs.
I turn real fast
  and hope to see
you standing there
  so close to me.
But I know you're gone
  and out of sight,
so I dream sweet dreams
  most every night.
Someday soon
  I will reach for your hand,
and join you forever —
  won't that be grand?!

Mary Warholak
Chinchilla, PA

I am an eighty-one-year-old widow. I have three children and one grandchild. I am a gold leaf artist and have hand painted on ceilings and walls in churches from the East Coast to the Midwest. I also like to write children's stories that teach lessons in life. I've been a Sunday school teacher, school lunch mom, bank teller and librarian. Between having children, I had many secretarial jobs. My husband and soul mate died twenty-five years ago, and that is what inspired me to write this poem.

Across the Way

What Is a Daughter?

She's sunshine in darkness.
She's a cloud full of rain.
She gladdens your heart
and eases your pain.

She's a rainbow of moods
that color your day,
but you couldn't accept her
if she wasn't that way.

An abundance of love,
the joy of pure laughter,
She's the beat of your heart,
the here-ever-after.

She's a princess in jeans
and a tomboy in lace,
with scrapes on her knees
and tears on her face.

She's the hope of all future,
the core of all past.
Guiding her footsteps
is a tremendous task.

How lucky, I, in this scheme of things
to be trusted by Our Father…
He gave to me a precious gift—
the mother of a daughter.

Artie R. Cross
Ripley, WV

Wild Horses

(When I was 20) Love is…….
Like the taste of melted chocolate on my tongue.
Wild mustangs thunder about in my chest on a prairie
(Where I believed my heart to be),
And where wildflowers grow abundantly.

Wretched it is for those whose wild horses have fled.
And whose flowers decorate only their dreams or their graves.

I shall always be in love,
For I will never corral my horses nor plow up the prairie.
Wild flowers grow where they ought to be
And where love blooms eternally.

(Now I am 60). Love's personality transforms over time.
Like a tetherball unattended, it slowly unwinds.
Where did they go, those wild horses? Has the prairie been paved?
No, they're just tucked in those journals where memories are saved.
I know in my head that love is still there,
Hidden in skin folds and diminishing hair.
In the silence preferred and the comfort of space
In a moment's glance, there is still a trace.
Ah, youth. It is so carelessly spent
And vanishes as quickly as last month's rent.
I still like the taste of chocolate on my tongue,
And corralling the horses, that isn't wrong.
With the passing of years, love's no longer blind.
Rather subdued, familiar and redefined.

Peggi Gray
Topeka, KS

You Still Love Me

After all the pain I gave you at birth,
You still love me.
While I was bad, cried and kept you up all night,
You still love me.
After the fights and names,
You still love me.
Even when I lose,
You still love me.
Although I wasn't completely honest,
You still love me.
No matter what I have done, will do or say,
You still love me.
I will always know that no matter what,
You still love me.
My life goes on because
You still love me.
I love you too.

Monica R. Esenwein
Sharon, PA

W.A.R. — Willing, Able, and Ready

Each morning when I rise,
Pride swells within my heart
'Cause I have the right to live
The way I want to live.

That right — thanks, I give freely
To my forefathers and Deity.
This freedom which I love,
May God bestow eternally!

Now, should you think it wrong,
That freedom is our right.
Hear this message strong:
We're not afraid to fight!

Some think war is evil.
Some think war is wrong.
While not our hope to wage,
It's freedom's worthy stage.

When freedom is at risk,
WAR simply means to us
Our country united will be;
W.A.R. — Willing, Able and Ready!

We won't let freedom fall.
We're not afraid to fight.
When freedom is in jeopardy,
We are W.A.R. — Willing, Able and Ready.

Kerry Moffett
Layton, UT

Across the Way

Goodbye. Hello?

Goodbye…
Insert the key and pull the door shut; pictures of days dog tired from an honest day's work.
Time for friends and play, to be.
So happy to be home.
Last word whispered the day life ended.
Must not give them the life of the spoken word.
Not when giving a voice would let the fear and sadness of a life ending.
What would volume realize?
I was never leaving; so found, a home, life.
Why close the door and drive into black night?
Don't go; you can stop this.
Turn around, your life's still here.
You can keep it all; stop this and turn back.
Flew far, far…
Too late…
all is gone.
Smile bravely and carry on; don't look back.
A time will come when it won't hurt and the missing will be replaced by the new.
Memories of hello, welcome are overtaken with hello, glad to have you.
You've come a long way.
I search for the way back;
it becomes my single-minded obsession.
Lost, probing, shadow seeking the way to hello, welcome.
Then into darkness a ray so faint, it's almost imperceptible.
What seems like end of days just a detour, the way to where I belong.
Hello?

Wendi K. Williams
Hanover Township, PA

This poem refers to warring emotions of sadness and fear, to leave my home of Fresno, CA (Goodbye) And the plan to one day return (Hello). Thanks, Mom and Dad, for making my bad choice bearable and for loving and supporting me, always.

Love

What is love?
Love comes from the depths of my heart. And is the strongest power of all.
And love can be shown in different ways.
Like giving someone a card that says a lot to make them feel better or being a friend to someone that doesn't have one.
But most of all God loves us. He loves us so much he gave His only begotten Son, Jesus Christ, to die on the cross for our sins.
God keeps me safe, wakes me up every morning, put me in a great family,
provides the food and water I need to survive, good clothes, and roof over my head.
And every single time we do wrong, He gives me another chance and another.
And He doesn't have to do all that for me. Jesus didn't have to die on the cross, He had never sinned once in His life.
But He had love to do all of this for me. And if He didn't love us we wouldn't be here today.
So the next time you think about love, think about how much God loves us, and all He has done for us to be here today.

Georgette Jones-Walley
Cordova, SC

Across the Way

Desert Light

I enter desert light each day,
I am challenged to look;
Examine myself in the bright.

Casting shadows
Are parts of me—
Secrets, addictions—
My personal demons.

I need to trust more
Be bold
Stop holding back,
Exposing secrets to light.

Only then will addictions,
The dark demons,
Have their grip loosened
So trust will replace the fear.

Barbara W. Grygier
Medina, OH

Morning Beauties

So early it was.
We seemed to stop in a shining light.
Trees we passed by sparkled so bright.
Ice covered the entire forest,
While birds sang a morning chorus.
The day was one I'll never forget,
The day with its beautiful features —
The ice, the light, the snow, the frost —
I know this memory shall never be lost.

Hailey Beckrow
Cass City, MI

TLC

Do you know how a gentle breeze
Can catch you by surprise
Or the smell of a fresh-cut rose
How the ocean's waves gently
Caress the shore
And the moonlight dances across
The water
How a simple smile can light up
The darkest day
Or a hug can overwhelm a heart
And condemn the soul

Tracy L. Mimms
Biloxi, MS

Across the Way

Flesh

My flesh is alive
  Let it die, let it die
Calling me taunting me
  Lord, let it die

Whispering from my heated loins craving consolement
  deep thoughts of kisses and spontaneous longings

Let it die, let it die

My nature is rising, naturally desiring
  but this is not what I need.

There's a battle between my spirit and my outer being
  Lord, let it die

I cannot let this carnality hinder me,
  physically and sensually have always been a major
  part of me… and all while my spirit was
  crying out so desperately; for me to be more like
  the supreme being who made me

Let it die, let it die
  Lord, my flesh is not who I want to be

Lord, I want my flesh to die
So I can live spiritually.
For my body is a temple, belonging to the King

Javon Winston
Richmond, VA

I rededicated my life to Christ almost two years ago, my desire to walk close to God inspired this poem. The flesh and its desires wage war against the spirit, which makes the sinful nature want to do evil. My desire is to do those things that are pleasing to God.

Untitled

In a little hand held so tight
5 little pennies shiny and bright
She wiggled and she jiggled and
Moved all around
But in that hand could always be found
5 sweaty pennies waiting to go
Into that basket with her face all aglow.
She's learning young, and it's good advice
What you give to God you get back twice

Helen M. Wall
Lawrence, MA

I am almost eighty-six years young. I have been writing poems since high school (1945). I also have written twenty-seven children's stories. Yes, I have been published in magazines and Weight Watchers newsletters. I am the mother of seven children, fifteen grandchildren, and three great-grandchildren. I write stories and poems that just pop into my head.

Across the Way

The Edge of Eden

We live on the edge of Eden,
Locked out of that grand place,
Our father's sins have cursed us,
To run in this endless race.

Perfection is within our reach,
Yet so far away,
Never shall we enter there,
See life inside its gates.

An ugly, broken people,
That is what we are,
Day to day we struggle,
To cover up our mark.

Nation to nation to nation,
One common thing we share,
We live on the edge of Eden,
And this is the curse we bear.

Brianna Carter
Lake Park, GA

His Love

I feel his touch like falling rain
calming my fears and easing my pain.
His voice like blowing wind
tells me he forgives my sin.

Seeing his smile in April showers
gives me hope in my darkest hours.
His warmth, like the summer sun,
gives me peace when day is done.

His love I feel when I kneel and pray.
It gives me strength throughout the day.
His song I sing in the silence of night.
It comforts me like dreams in flight.

Oh, the power of his sweet love
I see in the moon and stars above.
Oh, what joy to my soul it will bring
When I hear the heavenly angels sing.

Janie M. Durham
Cordele, GA

Other Love

He runs to her with a passion
And love that will not die.
Disappointments there are many
But he can justify.

I will always love him
Though at times it's hard to cope.
Like him I am tenacious
And will never give up hope.

I pray each time he goes away
That he'll come back to me.
This man is my husband
His other love the sea.

Darlene Honea
Burlington, WA

My Memories of Mother

A stitch in time saved nine,
What once was yours is now mine.
Old curtains made into party dresses,
Torn rags to curl your pretty tresses.
Wool coats braided into rugs,
Patchwork quilts wrapped you in hugs.
Crochet slippers, knitted shawls,
Patched up knees, muslin dolls.
Shoes worn out before their do,
Need cardboard soles shaped like a shoe.
Socks that had too many holes,
Were darned by Mom from heel to toes.
Young girls taught their sewing lessons,
Embroidered linens, framed house blessings.
Family heirlooms passed down through time,
Handmade by mothers dear and kind.
Of all these things I love the best,
was Mother's way she saved for less.

Cynthia King
Seabrook, NH

Eventide

As I watched the setting sun tonight
Gradually darkness replaced the light.
I watched the birds circling with beauty and grace
As they found a comfortable resting place.

I heard the last note of their beautiful song
As they settled in a stately Elm tree with branches so long.
The Heavens above were blue and clear
The stars one by one appearing, felt near
Yet, were farther away than I could see.

God's world is perfect
And I believe
He made it that way
Because He loves
Both you and me.

JoAnne Wentz
Napoleon, ND

God's Plan

Once darkness lay as a shroud,
Covering the souls of men.
Held tightly by the cords of death,
There was no escape from sin.

Until on a certain starry night,
Heavenly voices raised,
Piercing the silence of shepherd's watch,
Good news the angels praised.

Into the world the deliverer came,
Jesus was His holy name,
To conquer Satan, sin, and death,
Man's darkened soul to claim.

O, divine and wondrous plan,
Setting prisoners free,
God's redeeming love to show,
Bringing life to you and me.

Dolores House
West Fork, AR

Across the Way

Life Without You

Seventy years—
a lifetime—
When did we begin?
The many years have blurred the edges.
The sounds and smells are all the same—
They only miss your voice
(or the sound of your breathing).
We could pass many days in total silence
and never feel alone
(or neglected).
Becoming "one" is no myth,
though the merging is a slow process.
It is a mixture of tears and joys,
of trials and tribulations—
but we did just that
so, so long ago…
Now, as I sit here alone (am I?) with
my tears, I wonder if even death has
separated us.
I can feel you as though you were touching me
in the night. I hear echoes of you…
But then the old clock chimes and I'm reminded
of the present—the scent of you fades and the
tears come, the heart aches—
Life Without You—
  (Is there?)

Sharon Loney
Liberal, MO

Salute to an Artist

Norman Rockwell the artist his talents were rare
   Painting pictures of people with so much flair
Visitors come to look at his art
   At the museum in Stockbridge and hate to depart
His Four Freedoms arouse such a feeling of pride
   A salute to war efforts and many who died
The child of color walks to the white school
   Unforgettable faces in the Golden Rule
A boy pushes a carriage a baby within
   Runs into his friends who make fun of him
The runaway child and a policeman who cared
   Folks gossip together and act somewhat weird
Family going and coming on a great trip
No Swimming Allowed Here, but boys take a dip
The grandmother and child saying grace with such class
   Creating a picture which tugs at your heart
A license for marriage being quickly filled out
   and a clerk who was ready to close for the night
This artist so clever and witty and smart
   from Main St. Stockbridge he never would part
Presidents and movie stars posed for this man
   Come see his art whenever you can
A man with a vision who dared to dream
   of people and places not otherwise seen
Sing praise to America's artist so fine
   Be thankful he was a man of our time.

Margaret Williamson
Richmond, MA

My name is Margaret Williamson, my nickname is Meg. I am an interpreter of the paintings by Norman Rockwell and have worked at the Rockwell Museum for fifteen years. I am still in awe of the amazing art in the galleries. Norman Rockwell's art inspired me to write a poem about many of his well-known paintings. I enjoyed creating this poem "Salute to an Artist." My daughter, Heather-Rose, who lives in London, England encouraged me to enter my poem in the contest.

Across the Way

Winterlude Bloom

Eager breezes bound abruptly,
Seductively in winter thaw to turn a trick:
The moment melts into a new mood as old desires
And the unsettled seeds of promise seethe in the freeze.

December fades from memory in an instant—
Inexplicable forces in the skylit canopy cast a spell:
Birds appear in busy flight, filling every beak full
Of salvage from the snowmelt, repast of the Winterlude.

Sunstruck fires smolder in the whirlwind—
Sparks of the Winterlude Bloom ignite the earth:
Roots fuse and stretch their tendril tongues in thrusting
Frenzied thirst, diffuse, entwined for a bleak warmth, nude.

A few fluttering forsythia bend their arms aloft—
Bulbous windblown bud tips bask, swell, and burst:
The heat gathers luminous waves along a surging flux
Of streaming, sunswept blossoms, born of a midwinter tease.

Playful gusts whip the withered stalks erect—
Clouds of dust rouse the mire as matter grows to fire:
Cameos of crocus cups unfurl in the heat of bud,
Blooms of the Winterlude.

Rebecca S. Solon
Sedona, AZ

Rebecca Solon took American and English romantic poetry classes in a comparative literature program at the University of Michigan's Residential College in 1967. She graduated in 1972 with a major in the "History of Ideas," a combination of history, philosophy, and literature studies. Rebecca held professional positions as technical writer, copywriter, and as an editor-proofreader. On an unusually warm and sunny February morning in Northeastern Pennsylvania, Rebecca observed a snow-covered forsythia bush from her kitchen window. It was beginning to bloom! The yellow blossoms heralded a spring-like awakening of nature's forces, inspiring her poem "Winterlude Bloom."

Shackles Be Gone

I was one of many who took the test,
Math was a favorite and I did better than the rest.
The job at hand was mine for the taking,
But was that a mistake I'd be making?

Deciding to fill the hole in my soul,
High school graduation became my new goal.
After countless nights in adult education,
My reward was a degree and a new realization.

The head on my shoulders is really my bank,
All knew learning gives me more rank.
Filled with untouchable treasures all my own,
Layer upon layer my intelligence is grown.

My future now includes a college degree,
Teaching is my goal, ultimately.
Feelings of inferiority, less than and dumb have washed away,
Confidence, determination, desire and drive are here to stay.

With achievement and success upward I'll soar,
The shackles of "drop-out" will be no more.
A churning from deep inside has opened my eyes,
I will now look upward and reach for the skies.

Knowledge is the key that opens the doors,
Offers will come and the choice is yours!

Lucy Montoya
Platteville, CO

Across the Way

My Wooden Dream

It looks like at last the deep pain
That was somewhere in my soul
Was beginning to surface
And finally unfold.

A single tear fell to my feet
Unsteady as they were
When I reached out
Toward my never-ending dream
And tried to unlock my feelings
So that I could think and breathe again.
Now maybe my new life could take hold
And truly begin.

As he smiled at me until I could respond
I softly took "My Wooden Dream"
Oh, so longed for
And held it
Lovingly to my heart
Knowing my dear violin and I
Would never part.

Judith R. Parks
Norfolk, VA

Untitled

The world is a dark place, full of
Suffering and despair, but rays of light
Can still be found. In the smile of a child
The bond between a mother and baby
The pride a father feels when his child
First walks, the love between a bride and groom
On their wedding day.
Some are blessed with these lights
And will work to defend them.
There is another kind that observes the lights in the dark
Never knowing its warmth themselves.
Most serve the dark, but some stand on the verge feeling the
    warmth
Never knowing its full joy, these often fight to defend the light
Never having its joy for themselves.
Often I wonder where my feet stand
Not in the dark rage, minds of
Fog, blinding greed, or poisoning heart.
Nor fully in the light
All that is the light surrounds me but
Never mine. So does this make me the third,
One fated to watch and defend
But never have the light's joys for my own?

David Schuchardt
Cheney, WA

Across the Way

Dear Ones

I have been very richly blessed
Blessed from up above,
Blessed by the hands of the Master
And sent to me with love.

For God gave me the power
To write and understand,
The skill of writing words
On paper with pen in hand.

I write of friends and family
In miscellaneous topics I putter,
I write of heart-felt love
For my father and my mother.

I'm not particularly talented
It just seems to be God-given,
As far as the subject of poetry
It's a force that's strongly driven.

My heart is over-flowing
From night until the dawn,
Of adventures I wish to share
In my memory they live on.

So if you think I'm creative
As smooth as a clean white glove,
You've just given yourself a present
Sent from me to you with love.

Marty Massey
Omaha, NE

I Wonder Why, I Wonder How

Today is such a snowy day
  The wind begins to blow
Everything is on the move now
  To where…no one knows

The clouds are moving very fast
  And changing as they go
I sat and wondered why and how
  Don't guess…I'm supposed to know

The seasons come so quickly
  We can tell, by the birds that sing
Through summer, fall, and winter
  Nothing's prettier than the spring

Time is like the clouds
  Nothing ever does stand still
Only when we get to Heaven
  Will we understand the Master's will

So I'll continue to watch and wonder
  about all the beauty God has made
'Cause no one in this world can match
  The love and joy God gave

This old world and what it offers
  Even family and friends cannot compare
To peace and happiness we'll find in Heaven
  With Jesus, who's waiting there.

Brenda Richmond Gregory
Sevierville, TN

Living my life for Jesus is my main inspiration. Growing up near the Smoky Mountains outside Sevierville, TN, inspires me as well. We didn't have worldly riches, but we had what mattered most, God and family. I'm a widow of a forty-four-year marriage; one daughter, five grandchildren, five great-grandchildren. I am truly blessed. I will continue to write from my heart with the anointing hand of God as my instructor. May you feel His presence as you read these words.

Across the Way

Here's How It Is

Old age is golden ...
So I've been told.
But you know what?
I've yet to see that
Pot of gold!

However, I see its replacement
A lot every single day
As I take four water pills
And I'm headed that way!

Now taking two in the morning
And two more in the afternoon
Keeps me making a path
To the bath, across the room!
Oh, I'm thankful for water pills
I must confess
'Cause if I didn't take them
my legs would be in a mess!

So I'll end this verse
and say farewell
I found my "pot of gold"
in the bathroom as well!

Wilmetta Feezor
Indianola, IL

blue baby

an orange temple consumes
walls made of red—given in birth from blue
to presume this is so
shall lead without heed
to the profligate fury of One

one never made from the soft hands of men
but from enemies one's made small
hands made crippled
shall yield and be lost
as waves of a squall from the wind…

made from the outer most ripple of a pond
from the pebble too small to see
tossed without care or concern for the future…
the one from the hand of a babe…
hands grown but never matured
one's old but never new

hands that grow old and wise shall stand
tall against any storm
as long as they are cradled and guided and held
from the fold of the One to behold

Krista M. Groh
Bay City, MI

Across the Way

Geranium Music

It's probably not good to go back.
  But I need to be near the old house again.

The sagging fence that couldn't keep life out
still wraps the house with weathered arms.
Here and there, through its missing teeth,
high grass pokes its head to see the world outside.
They have hung a new gate —
  perhaps it will help.

There is a young woman on the steps.
She sweeps away geranium petals,
not knowing they are mine.
A lifetime ago I carefully tucked the tender shoots
deep into the warm earth —
  but their blossoms were short-lived.

I would like to sit with her on those steps
and feel the sun warm our legs.
We could sip our coffee
and drink in the taste of morning quiet.
I would tell her about the music of my house —
  the melody of beginnings and endings.

I want to share with her the soft strum
of laughter that once drifted from nursery windows,
the hum of busy lives that forgot to sing together,
the adagio dance on bed sheets that faded too soon.
And, of course, the soundless tears —
  I would tell her that's how I watered the geraniums.

Terry F. Forde
Carson City, NV

A Broken Spirit

I surrender…
The fatigue within my heart cries out for slumber
to release its anguish.

I did not enlist for this position I hold.
This war takes many prisoners, some chained to their condition,
while others are held captive by their obligation as caretakers.

There is an air of restlessness, which moves amongst the troops.
This feeling is shared by all who fight this hopeless battle.

The enemy is out there… watching….waiting.
It strikes when we're at our most vulnerable.

I've been respected and awed by civilians for my bravery.
Only the combat soldier who marches by my side can
ease the ache in my tortured soul.

The battle, fought long and hard, has regretfully left my
spirit in shreds, and scattered amongst the ruins.

While my child lay sleeping, a whimper escapes
his parted lips.

In an instant…
all thoughts of my surrender vanish, replaced by a
battle cry, to resume our fight with renewed vigor!

Kathy Cole
Canterbury, CT

Across the Way

The Origin of Life

In the midst of unimaginable science technology that channeled
research of the cosmos and put a man on the moon,
there is a ceaseless quest for the origin of life and debates of
evolution versus creation forever continue to loom.

The human cell is too complex to have evolved from primordial
soup some scientists are beginning to proclaim,
but their belief in their argued opinions the evolutionists and
creationists steadfastly continue to maintain.

The brain is a human computer sending functional messages to a
complex system of life-sustaining organs in the human bod,
So in conclusion that incredible masterpiece is undeniably
created by the master of the universe, the omnipotent God.

Vera R. Boyd
Denver, CO

Scientists' knowledge of physical world and lack of understanding human anatomy inspired my poem. The complexity of bodily systems with intricate parts working together to make life possible is proof of intelligent design. Human life could not "just happen" nor could it evolve from something coming out of the sea, and fossils are identical to live species today, thus questioning Darwinism. If humans evolved from a lower species, the lower species would have to have been created. Nothing comes from nothing and if everything "just happened," why is it not "just happening" today?

My Grandmother Is an Artist

I look at the drawing that I know to be a horse,
Do others just see scribbles?
My grandmother looks at my drawing and says that it is beautiful.
I am only 4 years old,
But I want to be an artist.
I believe that I can be an artist.

She teaches me to shape the lines into a head and body.
She looks at my picture and says that it is beautiful.
I say the same thing about hers.
I may only be 6 years old,
But I want to be an artist.
I dream that I can be an artist.

I practice and draw and sketch
It never gets old… but grandmothers do.
My grandmother looks at my work and lovingly says that it is
    beautiful.
I say that she is beautiful and hug her.
I am still only 12 years old,
People say that I am an artist,
I have been inspired by an artist…

Now I create my own artwork.
Though my grandmother no longer draws,
I still show her my art
And she always says that it's beautiful.
I am now 14 years old,
And I am an artist.

Gabrielle D. Walton
Ogden, UT

Across the Way

Tomboy

When I was young
I climbed rocks
and apple trees—
skinned my knees.

When I was young
I rode bikes,
made model planes—
played with trains.

When I was young
I hooked worms,
fished in a stream—
licked ice cream.

When I was young
I played baseball—
took many a fall
trying to play football.

Not quite so young,
I'm now a mother
reliving that fun
through my son.

Vivienne Hines
Bronx, NY

A Prayer to Our Mother Foundress

As you, my Venerable Mother Foundress
Dwell in God's Heavenly home,
I call upon your assistance
To help me be newly born.

I ask you for many graces
For greater love of God I need
So that on the way to perfection
Your words of charity I heed.

Let me be another Good Shepherd,
Hands outstretched to those who need me,
By being faithful to the little things
And performing all in love and simplicity.

Help my silence to be golden
As a chalice raised on high
And let my conduct be Christ like
So that others I may edify.

With courage, let me the right thing do
Though heavy my cross may be,
So that I may truly be of service
On this journey to eternity.

I close now with this little reminder
Of a prayer to God for me
That I may continue to live
With greater love and humility.

Sandra Sharon
Pittsburgh, PA

Across the Way

Jewels

I look in the sky of loved
ones gone by, stars glistening
and shining so bright.
Like diamonds floating,
and reflections of mirrors,
nothing short of a spectacular sight.
Clouds dancing in motion
and moving abound, every star
tells a story almost speaking
with sound. Crystal jewels
glowing capture attention
almost bigger than life
and worth every mention.
This infinity space that
mesmerizes us all is a gift
from the gods, makes a wonderful
call. As the day again turns
night and waiting to see,
I look in the sky of loved
ones gone by.

Nancy L. Granlund
Janesville, WI

Peace and Tranquility

A place so quiet, with grass all green,
Sweet-smelling aroma, surrounded by a heavenly gleam.
Ending hostility, placing harmony between,
Killing off hatred with love is serene.
Thanks be to God, for this heavenly dream;
Congrats, to your angels, winning battles unseen.
From one flower to the next, putting enmity to rest;
No matter the color life still exists.
Whether black or white, red or blue,
He can purify us all, one race, one group.
The blood of Chris makes us white as snow,
So fresh and so clean with a heavenly glow.
From the same soil, these flowers grow;
One says yes, the other says no.
Different directions these flowers go;
One gained the whole world, but lost his soul;
The other found Christ, finally to reach his goal;
Peace with God, on a Heaven-bound road.

Winthrop O. Boulware
Muskogee, OK

Across the Way

Happy 75th Birthday of Jean and Joan

J is for the joy that filled our parents' hearts J
E E and O were added just to help tell us apart O
A is for the admiration their doting friends expressed A
N is for the many nights we deprived them of their rest N

"Victoria" sounded so exquisite that to each baby they would give
the same middle name with which they'd have to live.
"Gold"a G and an O and an L and a D
were theirs to treasure and to keep
as long as they were single
until their true love they would meet.

One day Cupid found their hearts
and shot the arrow straight
for the "Gold-Dust Twins" had found
their loves and lifelong mates.

Everybody celebrates a birthday of his own,
but birthday joy is doubled
when there're twins like Jean and Joan.

Their last names may be different
and they live many miles apart.
Yet, every year in August,
the 13th remains dear to their hearts.

So, Happy Birthday, sister dear —
We've reached a 7 and a 5 —
and look forward to next year
when another birthday will arrive.

Jean V. Menking
Alice, TX

I was born with a Florence Nightingale lamp in hand! Nursing was my life's dream. Literary inclinations surfaced in high school. After seventeen years of academia, I earned the right to put RN, BSN after my name — dream fulfilled! Within three weeks I added on Mrs. to my name. After marriage and family, widowhood provided the intensifying of a dormant literary talent — not only poetry, but abundant diversified letter writing. However, love of music (playing piano, organ, singing) supersedes even the written word, music being the soul's pathway to Heaven. God's gifts of writing and music equal ultimate pleasure.

The Lion

Through the pathway God gives us that we may call life
Being a daughter or son, a husband or wife
There's a wilderness out there that sometimes we face
When we need to be held by a loved one's embrace
For the journey gets dark when the lion takes hold
And the results are not good from the doctor we're told
The fear and the wonder, they take full control
And you worry what might be at the end of the road
The lion, it roars and takes sleep away
And you're not really sure you can face a new day
The surgery takes place and the process begins
There's fear of the unknown, of how it will end
You pray and you pray till God gives you peace
And then through the darkness you feel a release
The lion keeps roaring and wants you to doubt
But you keep believing and tuning him out
You walk through the wilderness in hopes you'll get well
And friends all around you assure you, you will
This journey has mountains that you have to climb
Sometimes you're weary of its ups and downs
Then comes that day when the lion has died
And you feel new life deep down inside
And at the end of this journey the wilderness is brighter
Because you have become
A cancer survivor

Rhonda Essary
Bristow, OK

I have been blessed to have a loving husband of thirty-eight years and seven children. Now I'm the proud grandmother of eighteen, eleven girls and seven boys. The first poem I wrote was in December 1984, when I woke up in the night, after losing my six-day-old son, and the longest poem I've written was in 2003 after losing my seventeen-year-old son in a car accident; the poem was five pages long. My poem "The Lion" was inspired by the fact that I'm going through chemo — but through God's peace, I know I'll be a survivor.

Across the Way

Omniscient

I watch as I let my pen write on
I watch as it moves, halts and as the pen continues...
As if while seeing again my elusive thoughts
That once could have been there
Sometimes I envision those that still linger
If only for a brief fleeting moment
Awaiting that special future moment that lies ahead
Making plans to haunt and visit me then
While in a sane same instant of reflection
Bringing a brief flash of recall or precognition
So kindly allowing me a now
But when knowing that I see this
Then writes of my past instead
And patiently awaits while my future unfolds
Presenting itself as my now
Then so swiftly becoming my past
With my pen continuing still—to write on...
Until... *the end.*

Robert C. Lory
Burlington, WI

The Simple Life

Today the simple life can be found
with computers and gadgets all around.
To find the life of simplicity
the mind will hold the only key.
So close your eyes and let your mind flow
to another time that you may know.
It was simple way back when and
we would probably like to do it over again.
The trees were green, the skies were blue
and we didn't have a clue
of how our future would turn out to be;
we took for granted most probably
the simplest of times.
And now the only way to find
is to go back in our minds.

Cecilia Hattendorf
Hesperia, CA

I am a retired registered nurse and have worked caring for people most of my adult life. Writing is an outlet for me, mostly poetry. I love poetry and playing with words. Most of my poetry comes out in rhythmic rhymes. I have been blessed with many things, unfortunately electronics are not among them. "The Simple Life" was inspired at a time when I was transcending into the computer age, along with using my cell phone for texting and other electronic devices. It was, needless to say, an overwhelming period of time for me.

Across the Way

The Best Lunch

The best lunch I ever had
Had everything good, nothing bad.

My favorite fruit was served
Fresh peaches from the tree, never preserved.

The soup of the day was vegetable beef
With no peas or onions, to my relief.

The potatoes were mashed, salted and buttered
Can I have two servings, under my breath I muttered?

Steak well done can't be beat
At my house we call this "tall meat."

Cabbage fresh from the garden, sliced and diced
Finds a spot on my plate without a fight.

Get out the punch bowl and fill it to the top
Orange juice, lemonade, and 7-Up; I want a lot.

Homemade bread warm from the oven
I'll take six slices, maybe a dozen.

For dessert I want my mother to make
A chocolate, three-layer, frosted cake.

If this could be served to me, I would love
To thank and praise my Lord up above.

Kyle Leis
Wilton, WI

Settling Down

Settling down sounds like a chain swinging around my neck,
Evoking visions of the wings of a dove being bound.
It reeks of overness, it oozes discontent.
It tastes like the salt of the sea
And tears,
Because settling down
Feels like looking at the shadowed ground.
It doesn't feel calm, or safe.
It feels claustrophobic, repressing, boring, done.
Settle down, settle down,
Slowly now, settle down,
Until I shrink and whither,
Settle down until I can barely be seen
Under the hospital blanket.
Settle down until no one can hear my voice anymore,
Until I have no voice.
Settle down until the world forgets I'm here.
I close my eyes,
My breathing is too rapid,
My thirst for life too violent.
Settle down!
"Here lies a woman
Who refused to settle down,"
My tombstone will lie.
Because I did settle down,
Settled down till I died.

Juleigha M. Zeibak
Casa Grande, AZ

Across the Way

The Seasons

The wind is blowing fiercely in the crisp and frozen air and the trees are bending eastward with their branches all bare.
For the last of the brown leaves have fallen in the stiff breeze.
The landscape is absent of all animals born and the singing birds have long been gone.
Now that winter is drawing to an end, the bare trees branches will no longer bend.
Spring is finally here at last with all our friends the same old cast.
The singing birds, the animals too and green plants sprouting up all around you.
The soft breezes carry the sounds of nature from everywhere leaving you without a single care.
Summer will be here very soon with its clear skies hot sun and big yellow moon, that fresh smell relaxed feeling and lazy summer nights and all the stars shining bright, bright, bright.
Before you know it the leaves are turning brown and slowly falling to the ground.
Red leaves, yellow, orange and brown, all making a crackling sound.
Another summer has gone, a new autumn is born.
Red leaves, yellow, orange and brown slowly falling to the ground.

Ronald E. Honis
Teaneck, NJ

Untitled

As the sun slowly dies,
and the moon comes alive,
hand in hand
silence and darkness creep in.
The air is an empty glass
waiting to be filled.
For some it is as peaceful as a lullaby.
For others it is as suffocating as water.
The silence is calming,
yet haunting.
Shhhh.
You perk your ears
to find a hint of a sound.
You hear it whisper,
"You can't escape me."
You feel it welcome you
to its dark paradise.
The thing about silence is
whether you find it peaceful or not,
you are completely
alone.

Rachel Armellino
West Milford, NJ

Across the Way

Rain

It's what races down the windows
what cascades from the sky
what gives replenishment
to yellow fields below

It's life

So why is it called somber
why so bitter gray
why is it looked down upon
and sun is cheered hooray
why rejoice when rain is over
is it really bad!

When I look with hope
at clouds above
they hide in their shrouds
while I run and dance
skip and jump
feel droplets on my face
and smell that incense of beauty
I laugh with joy
till clouds are over
and realize
I am
alone

Saachi Grewal
Rancho Cucamonga, CA

To My Son

You must have been an angel
up in God's holy home,
and played among the stars
and sat upon His golden throne.

You must have thought I was lonely
so you came to be my very own.
You traded in your halo for
skeeters and flies,
fishing poles and mudpies.
Let me hold you to my breast
another moment yet before I put
you down to rest.

Thank You, Lord above
for giving him to me to love.

Marie Harding
Savanna, IL

Across the Way

Evaporation

I am nothing more than a glistening drop
of morning dew
being carried aloft on the satin wing
of a butterfly.

We float through the sweetness
of the white lilac bush
and glide by the stately towers
of purple delphinium.

Drawn toward a swaying patch of yellow daisies
we are suddenly free from the cool garden mist
and flutter on.

I feel the sudden heat
and I contract in the radiant morning sun.

I'm leaving my beautiful life…
I am warm and am no more.

Leza Lankford
Colora, MD

At a young age I loved to hear my mother recite poems, which encouraged me to write my own. As a teenager, imagine my delight when one of my poems was published in our high school newspaper. After high school I married, and we had two lovely daughters. Unfortunately, seventeen years later my husband passed away. In quiet moments during the busy world that followed, the long-ago joy of writing came back to me. I found much comfort and inspiration in this. The poem I submitted came to me in one of these golden moments.

Through Your Eyes, into Your Soul

Through your eyes and into your soul
They say so much, yet there's more untold
Through your eyes and into your soul
Ever changing, oh what a sight to behold

Sensual, exotic and timid but true
Rebellious yet grounded just to name a few
Subdued and seduced the first day we met
Stunned by your beauty, off my feet I got swept

Those eyes, those eyes, accented by your smile
Finished by your curves and wow those thighs
Intimidated and intrigued as I began to wonder
Just quite the experience of making love to each other

As our lips fused together and my body grew cold
The air went quiet, as I listened to your soul
For that moment in time, nothing else mattered
So lost in each other, it could not be shattered

Deep hard breaths as I exhaled from your kiss
No more hesitation as I reached for your lips
Wouldn't trade this instance, with you I'll grow old
In order to dive deeper, through your eyes into your soul

Jerone Scott
Jamaica, NY

Across the Way

My Christmas Poem to a Loved One

Christmas Eve—oh how can it be
  I so had a vision of you here with me
A quiet fire burning
  My head on your chest
With your arms around me in peace we would rest

A day that's so special to honor our Christ
  You and I giving glory for His birth that great night

This Eve you should know how much you are missed
  As I pray to the Lord for all on my list

For you I pray strength, and courage and peace
For the mending of hearts with no burdens to keep
For the spirit to guide you in all you're to be
And for you to feel the warmth of true friendship
  Sent always from me

Lisa Copeland
Crossville, TN

My Mother

She was a young girl who grew up
without a mother.
She had a lot of help from her sisters and brothers.

No indoor plumbing or running water,
her life was tough.
She learned that having a little was always enough.

She married young,
no father to give her away.
She had to be strong.
There were four kids to raise.

I know a woman
who is like no other,
someone special to me.
She is my mother.

Michelle M. Fraser
Springdale, PA

I Saw

I always knew him,
Or at least a little bit.
But in my time I'll never find
A man with sharper wit.
I saw in him a world of adventure,
I saw a world of fun.
I saw a place that will
Continue existing after he is done.
In that man, I never saw
A place where hatred grew.
In that man, I only saw
A blade called virtue.
I saw not in him, I think,
Even a single flaw.
Who was this man, you ask?
Well, I called him Grandpa.

Tanner Lloyd
Salt Lake City, UT

My name is Tanner Lloyd. I am from Salt Lake City, UT. I am seventeen years old and a junior in high school. I have a published book, Days of Sorrow and Joy, *and I'm working on more. I was inspired to write this poem by the fond memories I have of my late grandfather, who passed away at the age of ninety-three. I shared it at his graveside service.*

Weeds

A small reflection of the sun
There it was—a dandelion
Proudly perched upon the lawn
Now a weed to be disowned

Like the knapweed on the wall
At an exit, 'neath a bridge
Grasping life, its only soil
Crumbling mortar and old bricks

When weeds invade the garden
From the forests, fields or wind
Are their wild and wanton ways
Just thrown hither and beyond?

What about the weedy children
Lost in classrooms everywhere
Are they nurtured and protected
Loved, or treated with despair

Remember, they're the future
Artists, writers seeking truth
Forming the salvation
Of an overwhelming world

Merylene R. Schneider
Milford, MI

Across the Way

My Angel of Life

Through your eyes I see the window of time
The reflection of years gone by
Images of who I am and who I want to be
Hand in hand take me down the path of life
Just show me the way, close my eyes and dream
Through your touch I feel the love in your heart lift in me
The hardest part believing in me as only you do
Hand in hand take me down the path of life
Just show me the way, close my eyes and dream
Through your words the message I've heard
Live for today and let tomorrow be
Let time stand still for just a little while
Take things as they are
Embrace what comes your way
Hand in hand take me down the path of life
Just show me the way, close my eyes and dream
Through your love I have laughed and I have cried
Those are moments to be shared
What you gave to me I hope to give back to you
My angel of life
Hand in hand take me down the path of life
Just show me the way, close my eyes and dream

Annette Goodson
Janesville, WI

I think a lot about family and how my life has been influenced positively. The qualities instilled within are pieces of one's heart that have been graciously given, pieces that have made my heart whole and complete, and for that I am truly blessed. My mom is my inspiration. Going through life together, I wanted to express something meaningful and show how much I love her. This dream was made more special with the help of my uncle Johnny who touches one's heart with his beautiful voice and gift of music. He turned ordinary words into something extraordinarily beautiful.

I Can Only Be Me…

I can only be *me*, so why do I keep trying to be someone else

I can only be the *me* that God has put in place
The *me* that on one can erase

Why can't I see that in order to be *me*
I have to know *me*
I have to see *me*
I have to feel *me*
I have to do and be *me*
But most of all, I have to love *me*

When I imagine the small word of *me*
I must remember it embraces life for all eternity

It may take years for me to see myself
Or it may take seconds just to see what's left

So tread lightly when you're outside of yourself
Because when you are not you, you're really someone else

I can only be *me*, so why do I keep trying to be someone else
You tell me

You tell me

You tell me

Veria Franklin
Pittsburg, CA

Across the Way

Saved by Grace

"What is your name?" the stranger asked,
As He was passing by.
"Who me? Why I'm called Much Afraid,"
My brief but quick reply.

"Much Afraid? How very strange,
Who gave you such a name?"
"I gave myself the name, because
Deep wounds have left me lame!"

"This woundedness you speak of,
This lameness that you bear
Cast it all before your God,
He'll heal each wound with care!

"He too, has borne your woundedness,
He knows your depth of fear."
"Where is He, of whom you speak?"
"Dear friend, I am right here!

"Cast your fears into My Heart,
Each wound before Me place
When you do, dear Much Afraid,
I'll call you Saved by Grace!"

Georgeanne Farrell, FSP
Dobbs Ferry, NY

Channels

Just Add a Y

When I was eight, I was smart and sometimes sassy.
I was scared, yet somehow safe,
I could run faster than most girls my age and play a good game of boxball against the buildings.
I could sing soprano and be on key.
That made me popular with the teachers.
One of my favorite things was jumping double dutch for hours, such energy.
When I was eighteen, I was filled with confidence.
I fell in love and planned a glorious future,
Soon married, made a home, had a family of three and life continued.
I was still smart, not so sassy, but could still sing on key.
I learned much, lived each day and year—the good the not so good.
Taught English for three decades plus and kept a sense of humor.
I've survived with dignity—I think.
Now here's the adding of the Y.
No other decade can claim the same.
To eight just add a simple Y.
That's where I've landed, none the worse for the passing of time.
Still can sing on key and surely laugh a lot.

Ann Carlovich
Myrtle Beach, SC

Across the Way

Untitled

The light of now is leaving
And the gates of then are closing
As I listen to your breathing
And the peaceful night reposing

For this day begins a promise
Whispered in the early evening
As we discover now the feeling
Of a life that now has meaning

Robert D. Martin
Wadsworth, OH

These words were written in 1975 while I was in college and finding writing poetry more fun than engineering homework. Three years later I met and married my soulmate, Linda, and found out just how precognitive the poem was. I actually experienced the moment on our honeymoon. We've been married thirty-six years, with wonderful children and grandchildren. God works in mysterious ways.

I Do

Today, I make this vow
Today, I swear this oath
To be yours forever and evermore
To hold you close and never let go

When I look in your eyes
I can see our future
And I know that whatever comes our way
We'll make it through, fighting together

Today, I hold your hand
And my heart is complete
As we become one till the end of all time
In a promise that we'll always keep

Anywhere I will go
I'll be with you in health
I promise to be with you in sickness
Would take your place, should it lead to death

I feel deep in my heart
We'll make it through all things
I can't even say how much I love you
Baby, you make my heart want to sing

Today, I make this vow
Today, I swear this oath
Before God and man I declare
With everything that is in my soul

I Do

Keri L. Wilcox
Rhinelander, WI

I am eighteen, and when not working on writing my first series of books, I spend my spare time playing guitar and leading worship at my church, as well as composing poetry and songs. I'm inspired to write by things I see every day: a song I've heard, or maybe a phrase I've read. I have three siblings, and a niece and nephew, and this poem was inspired by my second oldest brother's wedding. What inspires me the most when I'm writing is my dream to travel to Ireland and wander the mist-shrouded hills and villages.

Across the Way

A Message from Fanny

Daddy Jim, don't weep for me
It's so beautiful here on high
I'm sitting on a fluffy white cloud
watching angels flying by

They play their harps and sing to me
in voices soft and sweet
They caress me with their angel wings
while I'm lying at God's feet

I did not want to leave you
because I knew you would miss me so
But when I heard God call my name
Daddy Jim, I had to go

The little boys and girls in Heaven were lonely
and needed a little dog like me
to run and jump and play with them
and to keep them company

Please get another little dog like me
so you can share good times like we had
Then you won't have to be lonely
and I won't have to feel sad

Daddy Jim, it's time to go
The little kids are calling me
They want me to run and play with them
and keep them company

Daddy Jim, don't weep for me
Daddy Jim, don't cry
The little kids and I are playing
With pretty angels in the sky

Lou A. Carey
Vian, OK

Silence of the Night

In the dark silence of the night
I can feel something near me
It cries and it grieves and is out of sight
Dreams are fears I do not know
The tears I shed within the night
My pillow soaking wet from fright
I will block the dreams of terror from my mind
Till darkness fails to be unkind

Katherine G. Otwell
Janesville, CA

My Blessings

Each time I take a walk outside for just a little while,
I always come upon a gift God gave to cause a smile.
The wildflowers, all so beautiful, He scattered here and there,
So small and delicate are they and bloom without a care.
The array is quite breathtaking and the fragrance is so sweet;
It seems so strange and wonderful to see them at my feet.
Then up above in trees now green with buds out everywhere,
The beauty of His Hand has come down Heaven's golden stair.
He swirled the clouds below the sky into a scene serene,
Of blue and pink and puffy white, it's all a painter's dream.
So when I gaze upon His work, so magnificent and sublime,
I know the handiwork is His, but the blessings are all mine.

Evelyn Dooley
Hull, GA

Across the Way

Purple Hat Ride

All aboard to fly and ride.
Using tokens of love to experience life.
A bit of joy packed safely without strife.
Tethered to a balloon, disappearing to the sky.

The Purple Hat Ride has a priceless sense of feeling and care.
Memories founded we will always share.
Mastering silly moments of crying and despair.
This ride can remedy all without compare.

But with all its wonder, the Purple Hat Ride can be the best thing
    to ponder.
With all its great grandeur, glamour and glee.
It can take you to a mountain, desert or sea.
The thrill of flight in a Purple Hat Ride — the greatest ride you may
    ever need.

Victoria Harrell
Clayton, AL

I was born and raised in a small town named Las Fresnos, TX. My parents were farmers. I married in 1993 to my husband, Robert Lee Harrell from Cairo, GA. We lived there until 2009. We have a lovely daughter named Veronica. We live in a small town named Clayton, AL. My inspiration for writing poems comes from our environment, object, events, dreams, etc. In this poem I'm expressing feelings of life.

King of Peace

Our Lord, the King, the King
of peace has come to
bless you with much joy
and love increase.
  May you find His gentle
handshake yours and love
and joy throughout the earth
  Take time to say
a prayer as He loves to
hear from you.
  Tell a friend how
great He is and give Him a
hug or two
  Never judge your love
to all in a monetary way, it's
the way you give it that counts
  Keep Jesus
always near.

Mary L. San Fillippo
Oconomowoc, WI

Across the Way

A Very Special Love

Old hands that shake, but still can hold yours
Ears that do not hear very well, but still can hear you call them
Eyes that can't see as well as they use to but still can see you
Slow arms that still love to hold you close to them
Worn and old faces that still love to smile at you
Old but loving heart that will always love you!

Paige J. Ussery
Georgetown, LA

The Nest

To my love,
who has flown silently alongside my life
with foresight and memory
gliding until death
We perch in solace,
with agile acuity,
on the fence.
Soar ever more
in the moonlight;
ruffled yet poised
sweet sounds of the night
Gliding amidst desperate souls;
always to return to the nest.

Julia M. Fettig
Wilton, CT

Channels

A Prayer for Your Home

Dear Lord,
Bless this home, and with Your light
Make every corner clear and bright
May their hearthside softly glow
So those who enter in may know
That You are with them in this place
To guide their steps and grant them grace.
May their cupboards full or bare
Be cupboards that will always share
Their humble door be opened wide
For weary ones to rest inside
Grant their hands, filled with care
To reach to You in constant prayer
My dear Lord of love and peace
Your presence with them never cease
May all the hearts of those within
Are hearts that have been freed from sin.
And their daily praises touch Your throne
For You alone, Lord, can make a home.

Patricia K. Ray
Augusta, GA

Across the Way

Stamp Stuck to a Letter

She is my true heart of happiness,
So full of love and laughter.
She devoutly says we are inseparable,
Like a stamp to a letter.

Now he does not feel the long distance
When understanding her close feelings at heart,
Only later to learn he accepts being
Her only stamp stuck to her every letter.

Today they endure life's burdens and pleasures,
As they remember becoming one union of love.
Whether it's close home or work afar,
It's always expressed with every stamp stuck
to every letter.

Paul A. Chromey
Plains, PA

Lord, Lift Me Up

Lord, lift me up, when I feel blue,
Tell me that I only need to trust You,
Trust You and love You with all of my heart,
So that I'll never from Thee depart.

Troubles and struggles are part of this life,
But we need only to look to Thee.
If things were too easy, we'd be led astray,
And from Thee wander far away.

Help us always to bear the cross,
No matter how painful it be.
With Thy help, it lightens the load,
And helps to make the darkness bright.

Help us to live by the Golden Rule,
All other children have struggles too.
Lead us to give a helping hand,
And always try to understand.

Lord, lift me up, when I feel blue,
Tell me that I only need to trust You,
Trust You and love You with all of my heart,
So that I'll never from Thee depart.

Arlene Mulder
Fremont, NE

Across the Way

My True Love

When I first saw you
I fell in love
And if I had wings
I would fly like a dove.
Because you have such a beautiful face
That I would do anything
To keep you in my space.

You will always have
A place in my heart
And that's something I knew
Right from the start.
I promise you
That I will always be true
And that
I will always and forever
Love you.

Andrea M. Grinstead
Heidelberg, MS

A Senior's Life

A senior's life, wow what a change
No cell phones, computers, or video games
No bathrooms or street lights, just running water indoors
In our little village, we had only one store

No Visa, Discover, or Mastercard
Only a tab when times got hard
We had a coal furnace with ashes and soot
No cars to travel, only by foot

Once a month, we would catch a bus
We stood and waited and made no fuss
We knew we would shop and get some new clothes
Jumpers and skirts, blouses and bows

But when we got home, we were so cold
My mom went to the cellar and shoveled the coal
We sat on the register and waited for heat
Then got ready for bed, in one bed we would sleep

It was hard times, but I wouldn't trade them at all
Ringer washers, no dryers, no dial tone to call
We took care of others, and were humble and kind
We lived by the Bible, went to church all the time

The world around seniors has changed so much
I hope in the future we don't lose touch
With love as the true meaning of life
The peace and contentment in doing what's right

Marsha Carr
Belle Vernon, PA

This poem is very dear to me, because this was my life. I was a coal miner's daughter, living in a coal mining town. We did not live paycheck to paycheck because miners would go on strike for months, standing up for what they believed in — mine safety and just conditions. They were hard workers. Also the mothers worked hard without any modern conveniences. They were always there for everyone making the best of everything. So seniors of yesteryear, a salute to you and all your hard work and sacrifices you made, to make a better life for your children.

Across the Way

Love Lost

Lost is what I get at such a cost;
seems with love I am lost.
You may give of your heart all too
soon, seems it happens with me, does it happen with you?
Please, please just give me a clue.
I have a love that can never be through,
it has all happened because of you.
As big as it is, it's not enough.
It's given and taken as though it's just a bit of stuff.
It makes me tired, it makes me weep.
Will there once be something that's mine to keep?
Tears fall down even in sleep.
Dreams are yours, forever to keep.
Thoughts and love, some there are no memory of.
They come into life, then disappear, as if on the wings of a dove.
What do you do? What do you say?
Will it all make sense someday?
Or... does it all just fly, fly away?

Mary E. Stearns
Jacksonville, FL

Child Mystique: His Royal Highness

It was of no mystery that He was of lowly betroth, preordained in
 divine truth,
The royal king came in a lowly manger from a mother of lovely
 manner.
Adorned by the heavens and the earth at the time of his birth—
A child so tender and gentle, yet His words were more powerful
 than
Thunder or any two-edged sword.
Neither the angels nor the prophets made any blunders about His
 birth.
In Heaven, He is the King of kings, on Earth, He reigns supreme,
 and, in death, He became immortal,
Most powerful, and broke the chains of death, thereby lifted off
 the earth and manifested in His father's glory.
He is our beacon in the midst of the storm, our advocate, today,
 yesterday, and tomorrow.
His royal priesthood is our portion; we are joint heirs through
 ransomed blood.
It is no mystery that many have rejected Him through conformity
 to the affairs of this world.
If we can follow our heart, the wellspring of life, we will be lifted
 with Him. His divine power
Given us everything we need for life and goodness through our
 knowledge of Him who
Called us by His own glory and goodness. We thank God who
 sent Him
Jesus of Nazareth, you are the greatest man that ever lived!

Margaret O. Nwosu
Waco, TX

My name is Nwosu, Margaret Oluchi. I am originally from Nigeria in West Africa and reside in Waco, TX. I am married to Levi Nwosu, who also hails from Nigeria, and resides in Waco with me. We have four children: Desire Ezindu, Praise Nnanyere, Promise Munachiso, and Destiny Cherechi Nwosu. My inspiration for writing this poem comes from the time of the announcement for this conception—which was in December. My thought was that Christ was the reason for the season, what would be a better way to honor Him than to pay a tribute to him in a poetic form?

Pulse

With each stroke of gray—
A singular, lettered smear.
Embossed upon dead, marked sheeting—
Unfeeling and blank without its face.
The scepter in my hand, mine, mine alone—
A dull, wooden trident-crumbling, silver trim…
A graphite tooth shielded by a fleshy, warming fiber,
And in my hand the years whisk by—
My scepter of past, present, future.
I travel wherever my rule transports me.
I fly with the words on the page,
And with the flick of my nail,
I flip the future—
Mandate the present—
Scrawl out the past—
My penmanship bleeding my experience
And by each passing syllable,
The words leave me, whole and yet scattered…
My bare mind exposed
And raw on the lines below.
My past recorded—
A listless, lifeless, sweeping leaflet.
Glowing with the life inside the graphite—
The pulse of the worded heart.

Tara Van Kleef
Lake Park, GA

"Pulse" was written completely and utterly on a whim. In fact, it was scrawled down in the midst of a mundane quadratics lecture in my sophomore geometry class. The poem really speaks for itself. It is an open and overt overflow of my love for writing, an explanation of why I cling to snippets of literature and their authors so tightly. Although I write openly, my scribblings have only reached a few sets of ears. Now perhaps my thoughts can grasp those who are a great distance from my own voice, and help them find theirs.

Make Me a Servant, Lord

Sometimes I wonder with the end so near
Will I stand up front or run to the rear?
Even though no one's going anywhere
We will all be judged now here or there.
I hope someday or even right now
If I was confronted, to kneel or bow
Will I be able to just say no?
My King's in heaven, He's all I know.
Lord, make me a servant,
Please be my friend.
You're the only one I can turn to.
When I don't know what's around the bend.
I've been such a sinner and the river runs wide
I'm so thankful for you, Jesus,
Even though You had to die.
We all used to wonder why things like this
Took place many years ago for our heavenly bliss.
We should all bow down to our Father above
Who gave His only son for us, whom He dearly loved.
And what kind of gift did we offer him
But shame and suffering on a tree?
I only wish it could have been me.
Please make me bold in spirit and in truth
So I can live my life just for You.

Carolyn J. Ross
Los Molinos, CA

Light and Dark

Light
Bright, enhancing
Hope and joy
Tunnels, fire
Light

Dark
Blackness, evil
Fear and death
Nightmares
Dark

Light and dark
Sun and moon
Mysterious, fighting
Never to coexist
Light and dark

Yin and Yang
Hope and evil
Daydreams, nightmares
Day and night
Light and dark

Charlotte George
Paola, KS

Untitled

Sometimes the mind lies down,
still
Like a fish stranded high on ground, yet
quivering, quivering
not yet dead.
Both mind and fish fatigued,
Shudder,
Desire that peace beyond things grieved, yet
struggling, struggling
Not yet dead.
Sometimes the tide shifts
And saves the fish.
Sometimes there is a sudden twist in kind,
And the marvel of awareness relifts the mind.

Nancy F. Kitts
Norman, OK

Across the Way

I Am From

I am from the pines,
Majestically shifting and dancing.
The occasional sparrow,
Disrupting one branch's rhythmic sway.

I am from wind,
Blowing my hair into an unsightly monstrosity.
Its low, hollow whistling,
None can compare.

I am from Billings,
Its endless horizon line.
I am from April,
Fresh dew, gleaming on the grass.

I am the reincarnation
Of another person, passed away,
Tied together by connections untold,
As they pass, I play; the card game of life.

I am from the clocks,
Hands face and heart.
As they tick and tock, I talk and walk,
Similarities that aren't all that similar.

I am from where, who what why how?
I am from past,
But I am right now.

Jack Person
Lolo, MT

I am a twelve-year-old writer, artist, musician, and athlete. This poem was inspired by confusion and questions, forcing me to think of who I was, where I would go, and what I am from. My family and friends are encouraging, and my dog is brilliant. Life is full of challenges, and even though some are simple, some, you never get away from. The more time spent with family and friends the happier you are, the more time spent in nature, the more time there is to realize the muses all around you, and from it, make master pieces.

Music 'N' Memories

Did you ever hear a song
That brings back memories,
Long forgotten in your mind
Crashing back like the roaring seas?
  When you hear a certain song
An old flame's face appears,
Memories your heart does find
That hadn't crossed your mind in years.
  The song reminds you of happy times
Or maybe a bad affair,
But no matter why it comes to mind
Those feelings show you still care.
  While your mind recalls those memories
Your lips can't help to smile,
For only you know how the song
Makes you feel for just a while.
  Why these memories linger
Is still a mystery,
The all-imposing hands of time
May be luring to set them free.
  So the next time you hear that special song
Just remember when...
Smile or cry to yourself
For the music did it again.

Patti Sliko
Johnstown, PA

Across the Way

Trees

Trees covering the land making a forest for the animals and giving shade for man.
Trees strong, tall and straight with brown branches and green leaves reaching for the sky.
Trees bold and bending with leaves and branches touching not letting you see through with the eye.
Trees with sparkling green leaves on branches waving slightly in the breeze.
Trees bending gracefully back and forth floating slowly over the golden fallen leaves.
Trees with wide branches and big leaves whispering to each other as the wind silently recedes.
Trees alone, bare and forlorn anticipating quietly for new life to be born.
Trees beautifully covered with ice and snow twinkling in the night standing waiting for daylight.
Trees all decorated with tinsel and lights waiting patiently for Christmas night.
Trees up on a hill standing in a row showing your glory to those below.
Trees at the river's edge soaking up the moisture as the waves gently flow.
Trees standing in the rain not feeling any pain.
Trees shedding all their leaves again and again.
Trees huge and grand with moss hanging from the large old branches that never sing.
Trees thin and still with pine needles straight and stiff showing crosses in the spring.
Trees changing with sights that bring wonderfully cherished delight.
Trees how magnificent you are through all seasons of the year!

Bobbie J. Howard
Brooklet, GA

Bobbie J. Howard, a Christian family woman born in Statesboro, GA, has lived in South Georgia her entire life. She has a bachelor of science degree in business administration and is a recently retired fashion and shoe store manager. This poem is in memory of her older deceased sister, Shirley Adelaide Jenkins Andrus, a published short story author. It is her first poem and her inspiration was received from her Lord Jesus whose power and mercy has shown in her life. "It was on a tree He gave His life and without His grace I would be lost."

Ode to the Wood

Maple
Arms stretched out over the ground
Fingers enclosed in a knotted hold
Weeds create the rings placed on these fingers
From past husbands
Dirt, water and sunlight

Her fingers creep under houses
Strong enough to tear them away from her precious home

Her body, tall and lean, sways to the song of the wind
She fights against hurricanes
But does not always win
And finds herself falling,
Falling,
To the ground
Where she lies
Broken and wounded
Waiting for death.

Her hair is free from all binds
Like Medusa's snakes
The strands are unpredictable
Like dreadlocks
With leathery bells tied to the ends
Leaves.

Animals find refuge on, around, and under her fingernails,
They live attached to her beautiful body
And nest in her hair.

Emily Perez
Wilmington, NC

Across the Way

Push

Take a second look at life. Flee for a movement and a better insight, the beginning of a better life is in sight. My second look tells me to take flight. It's like studying, taking notes, and reading books. It's got me up all night searching for an answer as to how to get my life right. I'm learning to put my priorities in order, because like a Coke machine with no soda I'll be out of order. Being in the same spot from year to year gets old real quick. Learning, making plans, and having goals makes me want to hop on a plane and take trips. In my world it's what you know and who you know that's what gets you far, with the help of the Lord you'll make it with bumps, bruises, and deep scars. Ambition and drive mean I have the potential; it's up to me to make the right decision, not give up when the going gets hard. Nobody is made in this world but we're all born, in a world that broken that's why we're all torn. Some of us have it better, others not so great, that's why it means so much to me to look, learn, and listen so one day I'll escape. I'm ready to take on what the Lord throws at me, God gives it to me, and he's going to put me through it because nothing in life comes free. Sometimes it's hard to hold my head up, and becoming a better person is easier when you're fed up. It rains sometimes but for the Lord I try to make all my days sunny, angels cry and so do I when life means so much to me. Imagining my dreams and setting goals to reach them takes me back to my track days of throwing hard and training, going steady and maintaining. Doing my best trying different methods and being progressive. I have the mentality that I am unstoppable and invincible, that no matter what the challenge I will persevere if I stay true. God follows me everywhere just in case my faith tries to crackle, I always
P>U>S>H
Pray. Until. Something. Happens.

Tasha Roberson
Bowling Green, KY

Angel

There was an angel in my life,
  We shared so many things,
Sea shells and sand castles,
  We flew through life on gossamer wings.

He taught me how to laugh and smile,
  How to run and fly through wind.
We were young and full of fun,
  But he only stayed with me awhile.

He left me with an empty heart,
  Filled slowly by life's journeys.
And though I know we were meant to part,
  How will I ever stop my yearning?

Elizabeth Potenza
Thornwood, NY

My poem, "Angel," is a reflection of feelings and memories I cherished about a very special person with whom, luckily, I was able to have in my life, if only for a short time. I have two grown daughters and three beautiful grandchildren who are the lights of my life! My passion is writing and I am pursuing it even more now that I have retired from teaching!

Across the Way
Moving West

It happened back some time ago
that we tired of all that ice and snow
And sweating in that high humidity,
So we packed our bags with all they'd hold,
jumped in the car and hit the road,
just looking 'round the country for a better place to be.

We searched the land both far and wide,
with the landscape skimming by our side,
'til we saw a sign that read "Young man, go West,"
So we followed it and whataya know,
we left that land of ice and snow
and headed for the prairie land to see what would be best.

We found this town and glory be,
we thought we'd check it out to see
if this would be the place we'd like to nest.
We drove right in and asked a man to show the way, and he began
to tell us which direction that he thought would be the best.

We arrived at the office just in time
to sign our names on the dotted line,
And a few months later we'll move in at last,
And when that glorious day arrives
in this new chapter in our lives,
We'll then begin to focus on the future, not the past.

The fun begins at daybreak with a round of golf, then later on,
we'll play a game of shuffleboard, and then
There's bowling and there's bocce ball,
and wait a minute, that's not all,
Tomorrow when the sun comes up we'll do it all again.

We love to feel the warm winds blow
so far away from ice and snow
To that land back East we gladly say *goodbye*,
From our back porch we can see the view
of Heaven with its reddish hue,
As the Arizona sunset lights a fire across the sky…

Willis E. Munson
Prescott, AZ

My Daddy

Daddy, right from the start,
You watched over me with love,
Holding me, caring for me,
With help from God above.

As I grew every day,
You stood beside me with pride,
Teaching me all you know,
And always wanting me at your side.

You taught me about Jesus,
And the way of our Lord,
You taught me to kneel and to pray,
And to not want for more.

Daddy, we still have a long journey ahead,
So as you can see,
When I grow up,
You are who I want to be.

You are my Daddy,
You were from the start.
You are my Daddy,
I love you with all my heart!

Karla Farrington
Malin, OR

Across the Way

Execution at Best

Behind the assurance lies curiosity.
The pain of not knowing is buried beneath.
I know I should trust you, and this feeling should pass.
Please forgive me now, please excuse my wrath.

Insecurities grasp my warm heart to death.
Why can't I move on, and have strength to repent?
Belief from within, shall help me to see,
The past is the past, let my present be free.

Should I be personal, and searching for vice?
Or do I forgo, and give your candor a slice?
I confess to you now, I'm fragile tonight.
My emotions are here, exposed in the light.

The thought to go searching through your mysterious act,
Don't worry it left, without any slack.
My eyes are wide, but my mind's settling now,
In goes the towel that was holding me down.

Behind the assurance lies a soul lost in fright.
Let the past disappear, and the present be bright.
No more pain and no more concern.
You're not who he was, it's you that I yearn.

I'm sorry for the reluctance and the lack of belief.
I love you to death, like a heart skips a beat.
Understand when I say, this trail has burned.
Execution at best, believe me, I've learned.

Kara L. Magill
Helena, MT

The Last Explorers

As bloody footprints scorch the sands of the Elysian Fields, I walk in jest knowing that the sirens sing my epitaph along moonlit tides, and erode our lives into the limestone cliffs for the human eye, these men, who were almost heroes

I quaff alone tonight on tap from the Okeanos to quench a thirst that didn't need quenching, and fill a well where the water ran clean,
Until the word comes from Isabella or God himself I keep on walking

I look to the thunder above as I hear my men flee, their screams pierce the sky,
Unstitching the fabric of immortality, we were born resting comfortably on the palm in the left hand of God

Men of fate lay weary knowing not where or who they belong to, but knowing that their time is short lived. I can assuage your pain with purpose if you follow me for just a moment longer

Promises made as fluid as Ponce and Herodotus, now only your tears may baptize you anew as we tan by the Pool of Bethesda, bound to one another by oxygen and prayer, trust me like your own newborn, and care for me as tenderly

Joined in despair by wordless men masked with unrecognizable faces
We walk now together, are these my brothers? Are these the men I am meant to trust? Is my face masked by the same fear and compromise? No

In the name of the Queen, and with my heart in my hand, I walk deeper men,
I walk deeper, deeper into a void of nothingness, deeper into fear,
Because we are not done yet, follow me a moment longer, and let's be the heroes we were always meant to be.

Daniel T. Larson
New York, NY

Across the Way

Granted

Granted we were born and we will die
We may fail even though we try
Sometimes we win, sometimes we lose
We will pick and we will choose

Granted we will crawl, walk and run
We will cry, laugh and have some fun
We will do things right, and do them wrong
dance our dance, sing our song

Granted we will see darkness and the light
We will walk away from trouble, sometimes fight
We will be up, we will be down
Wear our smiles, show our frown

Granted you will have friends, enemies too
hopefully more friends, enemies are few
Sometimes seem rich, other times poor
at times you act selfish and always want more

Granted you will have sickness, remember your health
when having hard times remember your wealth
wealth in your family, friends, and God up above
given in faith, hope, charity and love

Granted you will love, you will hate
until the end know not your fate
Granted God will hear you pray
and grant forgiveness Judgement Day

Anna M. Sparks
Meadow Bridge, WV

The Rise of Fall

The summer has passed;
it's now in the past.
Here, right now, fall is in the cast.
Leaves from the trees do now fall
As autumn's pasts do I recall.
It's now the time the air is crisper.
No noise from the wind, not even a whisper.
Fall now has arrived
(Thank God I'm alive)
for the Rise of Fall
And the season when you we will soon recall.
Yes, summer fell from our midst
Like the morning dew and also the mist.
To many people, summer yet will be missed
But I myself do enjoy the Rise of Fall
The time I enjoy (yes) most of all

Nelson N. Shook
Pittsburgh, PA

Across the Way

Happy Mother's Day

If it's anyone you love and the one you love the most
I choose my grandmother, because we can laugh at everything that is gross.
You're going to have to travel through your heart and the emotions you feel
Find the feelings that are so exhilarating and the ones that are so real.
If it's anyone you love and the one you love the most
I choose my grandmother, I love her and we are so close.
She has been my guardian angel and my savior
She's one to love you with problems and failure.
She is the most beautiful person I know,
And sometimes my appreciation is absent and difficult to show.
No one really knows what all she does for them because she doesn't need the praise
All the time she spends for them, worrying and working for days.
If it's anyone you love and the one you love the most
I choose my grandmother, because she is the perfect host.
I can see when it hurts her but I know there is nothing I can do
Her pain for others is something I wish they knew.
She is the one I look up to, and the best person I know
And the relationship we have is something I will not risk to blow.
If it's anyone you love and the one you love the most
I choose my Grandmother, because she is the perfect dose.
A dash of kindness, a pinch of laughter, a spoonful of patience, and a gallon of love
She is most recognized from the heavens above.
I'll love her through it all, because she is my hero
And I hope she will read this and takes the time to be thorough.
If it's anyone you love and the one you love the most
I choose my grandmother, well, because she is *mine*.

Alicia D. Briseno
Riverdale, UT

Counting the Years

What is age except just another number?
Seventy or seventy-one doesn't mean you go into a slumber!
We may not have achieved great wealth,
But isn't it better to still have great health?
When we are asked to go the extra mile,
We can still do it with a smile.
All of a sudden you're facing seventy-two!
You might shed a tear or maybe a few.
You start thinking what's it going to be,
Now that you are facing seventy-three?
What is this thing about one's age?
Does this now qualify us to be a sage?
There are many having reached seventy-four,
Who say "Oh my God please no more."
The alternative doesn't look so hot,
So why not give it another shot?!
This is the time to enjoy life, go seeking.
Looking into your inner self, not just peeking!
It's amazing how time keeps zipping by.
Occasionally you might heave a big sigh.
Keep celebrating each day
In almost every exciting new way
Because if you can still survive,
You will pretty soon be seventy-five!
Happy Birthday!

Nancy Willen
Mahwah, NJ

Across the Way

White Magic and the Old Mutt

The magic of the season's first snowfall has begun.
I listen to the silence from the sliding glass door.
The flakes erupt into prisms of color
as they dance around the deck light.
The old black mutt nudges me gently.
He steps out onto the deck, nose pointed up,
sniffing the quiet air.
He looks back as if to ask
"Do I dare break this beautiful silence?"
I say nothing but motion him on.
He leaps down the steps, leaving behind him a
puff of white powder and another scattering of
colored prisms.
I ponder childhood memories,
snow angels, sledding, wet mittens, hot chocolate.
The old mutt returns, tail wagging,
happy from his brief excursion.
His tracks already covered by a carpet of the
white magic,
as if it did not want its silence disturbed.

LeAnn Crawford
Lynch, NE

My Travel

The signs are broken
And here I stand
Waiting for the bus
That passes by

Looking through the window
I could clearly see
A faded painted store
That used to be

The bus had stopped
Some had gone
To meet their loved ones
I continue to travel on

Winding roads extremely steep
Dismal, and dangerous too
Rough, somewhat bumpy
Like a tornado had passed through

Out and into a better zone
Making stops, bidding goodbye
Turn around, no one was there
Only the driver and I

My destination had reached
My host out of sight
Into the darkness
Left without a light

Beyond yonder and far from
Crimson lights are turning on

Barbara Singh
Woodhaven, NY

I was born on the small island of Trinidad and Tobago. As a child, I loved reading poems. My inspiration came from my dad, who loved to read everything. He wrote little poems to my mom before they were married. When I came to the USA in 1982, I was interested more in writing poems. I am writing and will continue to write—it's an inner satisfaction.

Across the Way

Our Flag

I look out the window each morning to see
That red, white and blue just-a-wavin' to me.
If only my camera could capture this sight,
And the feeling I have when I look at this delight.

She flies with such power, yet dignity too,
My words just can't describe this red, white and blue.
At times, her fabric's whipped by the wind —
Like a test,
Then in the nightly shadows, I see her hug the pole —
for a little rest.
I know she stands for liberty and justice for all,
And she'll always respond to each needy call.

So thanks to my neighbor who maintains this beautiful scene.
But then, what else would you expect from this big, retired
    Marine.
And a salute to all military, past, present, and to come,
For they do a job respectfully, that has to be done.

Well, my coffee cup's about empty, so it's time to start my day,
I'll try to do my best 'cause that's the American Way.

Ann T. Pagliai
Spring Valley, CA

Snow-Blown Resolutions

I heard the sound of voices
The joyful gathered in the square
The first to bid on a brand New Year
But "let the buyer beware!"

Resolved, some promised to spread the love
and show warmth towards their fellow man
A generous notion to better this world
But the polar vortex had other plans

To shed those pounds and join the gym
The terminally overweight swore
But after weeks of shoveling snow off the ground
Exercising became a real bore

No more lateness for us, the multitudes cried
We'll be at our posts before nine
But with snow falling down, no trains could be found
Just broken promises stranded on the line

By month #2 they all had "de Blas"
Blizzards made "vision zero" the norm
New Year's resolutions frozen in ice
Six more weeks to weather the storm

We may sometimes feel like two cities
But we all share the blanket of snow
The new mayor has big plans for the faithful
But for now Mother Nature runs the show!

Alice Maddox
New York, NY

Across the Way

God's Handiwork — Trees Along the Highway

An almost endless array of design:
As many styles as there are miles!
  Heavenly collage of shapes, colors, hues
Seemingly endless depth and length
  Separated by splashes of human construction
Variety in craftsmanship:
  Majestic — standing tall and strong
Silent sentries of the road
Life-sustaining:
  Some bearing fruit; all producing oxygen
Artistry for the eyes
Infinite wisdom on display
Its beauty reveals His love and grace
Adoration and appreciation swells the heart and inspires awe
The work of Your hands flowed from Your fingertip with ease.
Appears effortless, like the strokes from the paintbrush of a skilled
    artist
Seemingly random, like a Great Gardener who spread a handful of
    mixed seeds in one fell swoop.
Yet, I concur... actually, must be deliberate!
Your purpose: Surely Jah!
Must have been to summon this response:
"Reverence one must offer!"

Deborah Gordon
Brooklyn, NY

On a little getaway trip for relaxation and a diversion from the everyday grind, I was moved by the beauty of the fall foliage to pen this poem as an expression of my awe and praise to the Creator for his wonderful works! No matter the situation, you can use the opportunity to give thanks and praise!

Incomplete

Typically it's unlike me to let you in this close, but
I've been cast in the wrong light, so there are some things you
should know.
Let's begin at 5 years old, in a city full of potholes,
in a single-parent home
without guidance or rules to follow.

Just a mother with her bottle, cussing the man I role modeled,
because he left her with a young boy to coddle.
And that's the reason I'm hollow
and can't see a better tomorrow
'Cause every day for me left me drowning in that sorrow.

So what was I to do but pick my own self up?
Even if I was too little to know what my own self was,
I own that myself.
They say acceptance helps, but truthfully it never quelled the burn
in my steps going through hell.

But I guess that was life forging me into this man I've become.
I was forced to run the streets; it's the only place I found love.
So forgive me if I don't meet the standards of who you want me to
be.
I'm still a work in progress,
Waiting to be complete.

Jason Pagan
Marlboro, MA

My inspiration for this poem "Incomplete" comes from the dysfunctional childhood I grew up in. I was trying to paint a visible picture that would allow the reader to capture my fears, pain, and hopes.

Across the Way

Ode to Earth

Behold this fertile land.
Soil-rich, furrowed,
and spring-time plowed.
Wed in fidelity
to pine, birch and
apple tree blossomed-bowed.

Birthed from heat and dew,
this promising land.
Fruitful, juicy,
sustained by caresses
of a human hand.

Rain-drenched and airy;
parent of all prolific things,
this sod.
Praise shouts to Heaven;
praise be our planting God.

Seed-fed, this earth;
rich in soil, lumpy and lush;
hand turned and tended,
peopled with tree, shrub and brush.

Behold this fertile land.
New life spring-time sowed
in rain, sun and seed.
Praise be to Him
who sows our every need.

Carol A. Bearss
Boyne City, MI

My Fight's Not Over

Every three months I go for a test
I don't know whether to cry or be blessed
Sometimes I'm healthy, some days not
I tend to forget what I got
I'm not afraid of dying, I know God's there
But leaving behind all those that care

I have a brother and sister and two grandchildren I adore
A grateful husband and a daughter I love even more
God says there will be a cure, I leave it in His hands
Don't live every day as if you were dying
But live every second as if you were flying

At the end, I had good news
Nothing was found, and I was totally confused
Only God could have made this right
He gave me the courage to stand up and fight

Aida Yaccarino
Leesburg, FL

Across the Way

On Skipping Stones

A little flat rock wanted to fly
across the waves so high
but he rested in the sand
until a little girl gave him a hand.
With a gleam in her eye
and a bend to the right
into the wind she gave him a spin.
The little flat rock skipped and skipped
to a refreshing dip
waiting to be chosen again,
and like the starfish story
become an allegory.

Donald C. Lee
North Kingsville, OH

For over forty years I have been a writer and an educator. This year I will reach seventy years as a dreamer looking for my next skip 'n' spin to raise the ante when I win. My wife and I have been blessed with four boys and have always looked to life's experiences to inspire and motivate them.

Bringing Her Bones to Light

Judy rode her horse under the blazing
branches of late October, going slowly uphill
to heaven ahead of me.

I saw, though she was dying, her heart
beginning to glow from inside out, the oaks
a pink movie of western light

over her as she leaned into the saddle,
lifted out a miniature Coors from the pack
at her side. The horse swayed a little

and the ground grew spongy beneath them.
Her thick hands fluttered like swallowtails,
one of them lighting on the horse's

mane, wavering there, stunned
in pure silence — waiting for the tune —
something secret and still,

that would make light of this life,
this heart burdened, would let her rest
from the way her mother ignored

the torn moon that etched her forehead.
A squirrel shot across the path in front of her,
the horse shied, the broad haunch righted itself again,

not rotted, not surrendered, but wading
through all that fallen light
on the way to dust.

Catherine Ferguson
Galisteo, NM

I have been a painter and poet all my life. I have mostly made my living from my paintings. In addition to watercolors and oils, I make "retablos"—paintings of saints on wood, a New Mexican tradition. My parents were both artists studying art in Mexico City when I was born in 1947. I live in a small village outside Santa Fe, NM, where I love to garden and walk my dog. I have become interested in writing about my family. My dear Aunt Judy, who died in 1979, was the subject of my poem "Bringing Her Bones to Light."

Across the Way

The Leaves

I sat on my front porch today,
Watching some squirrels and birds at play.
It was warm and mild, early fall,
I heard a soft, sad mourning dove's call.
Across the road were goats and sheep
They had no appointments to keep.
A breeze went by, on its way to town,
And the leaves came a tumblin' down.
So here we are, once again,
Another year has reached its end.
It's harvest time, the crops are in,
Whether we lose or whether we win.
Things are different and yet the same,
We play the rules of life's great game.
Whether we smile or whether we frown,
The leaves come a tumblin' down.
Oh, they'll come back, most of them,
When Old Man winter gives way to spring.
But some of us won't be around,
When next the leaves come a tumblin' down.

Garry Owens
Lebanon, TN

When I Think of You

When I think of you, my friend,
I think of days long gone…
Of crazy days and carefree ways,
Bike rides swift and races won,
Laughter, loud, and bold and daring fun.

We were growing up and facing fears,
Having doubts and shedding tears.
I remember long, long walks
And endless conversations…
The songs we loved and harmony we sang.

I see the mountains towering there
So near and yet so far,
Beckoning the hikes so bold
Along their rocky ledges,
And think of rivers waded icy cold.

And then one day the magic of our lives
Began to wane.
Our paths became our own and flung us far;
To love and grow and find whatever dreams
We may have sheltered way back then.

Now beyond those years we've found reunion;
Memories of friendship flooding through.
And though the miles still are far between us,
We have whatever years will kindly give us
To share those old sweet times, just me and you.

Billie Scheel
Sun Prairie, WI

The Golden Butterfly

The golden butterfly on my lapel
Has a story to tell
Mark was only four
Don was faraway fighting a controversial war
Granddad to Mark, young man let's go to the store
Hand in hand, they disappeared through the door
Christmas morning
A cold clear day dawning
With a smile on his face and a sparkle in his eye
Open it, Mom, I wrapped it myself
Not Santa's elf
The golden butterfly
A story of sacrifice, love and joy
A dad, granddad and little boy

Mary Ann McKinney
Hanford, CA

I grew up an only child with lots of cousins, mostly in Oklahoma. I have been married to my husband, Don McKinney, a retired naval aviator, for fifty-eight years. We have one son, Donald Mark and one granddaughter, Quinlan. I wrote "The Golden Butterfly" from memories of that Christmas so long ago. I treasure the Monet costume jewelry golden butterfly even more now that my dad is gone and my son is grown. My husband is my most fervent supporter. The writers group at the senior center in Hanford, CA, encourages me to write, as do our son and granddaughter.

Ravenswood

Ravenous the heart of the black bird
winding through tall skies
where no simple need is not met,
where no life is too small
that it is not watched over, lovingly;
where no crumbs fall,
but they are lifted and with strong wings
brought back to the ravenous young
waiting in the brooding dark,
secure in the nesting place of the heart.

She will follow the hunters: the wolf, solitary,
or in roaming packs; or now the humans—she waits
and listens, keen to the gunshot sound
that triggers the death that comes but once.
The knell has sounded: a roaring echo through the
hallowed woods, and she leaps from her snowy branch
and glides toward that place
where the living meet the dead.

Feeding now on tender entrails
in the smoky time of day,
in the short months of our lives,
long past the time of fear—
and calling for others to share the feast.

Allen Van Etten
Brownsville, OR

Across the Way

American Values

The lesson learned each time we strayed
From apple pie and lemonade
From standards and conditions we fought to win
We had to bring back American values again

We the people go to any length
Eternal vigilance courage and strength
To hold the freedom we cherish most of all

Our forebears wrought the liberty
To seek our own prosperity
Our happiness as we pursue our dream
The founding fathers laid out that fateful scheme

And Americans chose the rule of law
Under a constitution we hold in awe
With a bill of rights to ever guarantee
Equal justice shall prevail for you and me

American values go to any length
Eternal vigilance courage and strength
To hold the freedom we cherish most of all

At times we loosened our grip but we held 'em still
And the good Lord willin' we always will
They're ever the same in a mansion or a shack
We'll always bring American values back

Lois Agee-Herring
Middletown, MD

Pet Termites?

A friend gave me termites to be my pets,
That was the strangest gift he has given me yet!

I wondered what I would do with this glass cage,
Of tiny creatures that would put Mom into a rage.

My little brother was so intrigued,
He decided he wanted to help me.

So he sneaked them into Grandpas room one night,
They all escaped, they were nowhere in sight.

We searched for them day after day.
During that time, I learned how to pray.

I knew that Mom must not find out,
Or I would get a lickin' no doubt.

One day we noticed Grandpa walking funny,
He had a hop in his step like a three-legged bunny.

Scratching and clawing at his pant leg,
He sat down at the river's edge.

When he sat down to take his wooden leg off,
We knew right away what had made him scoff.

There were holes all through his limb made of wood,
It was those termites making him scratch as hard as he could!

What a mess I made of things this time,
Just trying to be nice and ever so kind.

From now on, I will be honest on the double,
And refuse any gift that would cause so much trouble!

Alice K. Lee
St. Paul, VA

Across the Way

Remembrances of a Lifetime

I sat with my Dad every night,
since I didn't want him alone when he saw that bright light.
Some nights we would just talk,
and on others, we would pretend he could walk.
He would take me back to the day
when he was combining and bailing hay.
This was hard work from what I hear,
but to Dad, this time on the farm was very dear.
He had stories of his team of blacks and his brother's team of bays,
this was vivid in his memory, when today's thoughts were just a haze.
Then we would talk about his sisters and the pranks he'd pull,
oh how he would laugh until his eyes had tears so full.
But when we talked about his life,
it always included Mom, whom he loved for many years as his wife.
My brother was who he always wanted to see,
even on the days when he could talk to me.
With all of the good times, some of our talks were sad,
like when I told him it was okay to go and none of us would be mad.
Together we both shed many a tear,
not for death, but for all of the unknowns that we did fear.
During this time I made sure to tell him things from my heart,
that I loved him, was proud of him, and would miss him once we did part.
Finally Dad's breathing did stop,
and I watched as the curtain of Dad's life did drop.

Sheila Maxwell
Rushmore, MN

Little girls have a special bond with their dad. This was also true between my dad and me. As I grew up and my dad grew older, that bond became stronger. When he was diagnosed with cancer, I spent a lot of time with him. The night before he died, I was sitting alone watching him sleep. I began thinking about his life and all the stories he told about it. I then wrote this poem and read it to him before he passed away.

A Matter of Perspective

Gravity has suddenly become an appealing strain
Instead of something to rebel against, to reject, to defy.
There is new ground to be broken, experience to gain.

Though the earth's draw has long seemed to be aviation's bane,
A time comes when one unearths matters closer to the heart than
    the dream to fly.
Gravity has suddenly become an appealing strain

To bring a man tighter to the earth than Prometheus' chains.
As if an instinct has unexpectedly emerged, the mind stutters, the
    body complies—
There is new ground to be broken, experience to gain.

Turgid stems twist, budding flowers succumb to the sky's clusters,
    swollen with rain.
Earth's shifting pulse provokes the heaven's response, this
    poignant, piercing cry:
Gravity has suddenly become an appealing strain.

A voyeuristic facilitator in fact, allowing the frenetic forces an
    exclusive lane
To rush against one another wherever creativity persuades them
    to pry—
There is new ground to be broken, experience to gain.

Now flight seems nothing but a hasty conceit, a notion spawned
    in vain.
Pushed aside by the grasping roots of the present, intertwined in
    one enduring sigh.
Gravity has suddenly become the appealing strain,
There was new ground to be broken, ah, experience was gained.

Ben Walker
Charlotte, NC

Across the Way

Petals of a Fallen Rose

Petals of a fallen rose
I will gently gather
wishing somehow I could arrange
in nature's fashion
a beautiful restored flower,
ever blossoming,
ever fragrant
as I remembered.
Ever will I hold on to
those withered remains
close to my heart,
within the chalice of my soul
knowing in God's radiant worlds
nothing truly dies,
but changes
and grows into something
even more beautiful
in time...

Mary Ann Zumer Reese
Weirton, WV

Pink Princess

Pink lemonade
Strawberry shortcake
Ketchup on pancakes
French fries with syrup
What if the world's pink
What if I dye my hair totally pink
(Girl, pink is so cool.)
What if I wear a pink bikini
What if I go for a massage
What if I fall in love with Prince Charming
Ah… Ah… Ah! Oooo…!
Pink Princess
Heck! I want to be a pink princess
Waiting for true love's kiss
Waiting for Prince Charming to ask me out
And to stay a virgin until I'm married. Go girl!
Pink princess gown
Pearl earrings, lipsticks
Pink heart-shaped necklace
Pink purse and high heels
Will I be so rich…God
Will the world be good, no more awful wars, homes for the homeless
Will I roar, vomit, faint, or freak out
Will I be a princess for real
If my Prince Charming asks to marry me
Ah…Ah…Ah! Oooo….!

Rosaleen K. Nguyen
Garden Grove, CA

I am Rosaleen Nguyen. My ethnicity is Vietnamese. I have six sisters and four brothers, including myself. I love my family. They are inspirations for me. I want to do something to change the world, to make the world a better place to live. So I came up with writing a poem — "Pink Princess." I hope "Pink Princess" can bring joy to people and bring change to a better world, a world of peace. Another dream is to have my children's story Princess Kim *published and sold in Barnes & Noble. In memory of Dad. Thank You, God.*

Across the Way

Mother's Hands

A mother's hands do so many things
Besides remove bathtub rings.
They cook and scrub and clean,
And everything in between.
They make the bed and soothe a fevered brow.
They even milk a cow.
Hands that wash and iron and darn your socks
And then trim your unruly locks.
Strong, working hands to make your burdens lighter,
Gentle hands to make your life brighter.
Comforting hands full of love
Given to mothers from God above.
I penned this little rhyme
In memory of that dear mother of mine.

Lynda R. Young
Waldo, AR

At the age of thirty-four, my mother became a widow with five children, ages nine to fifteen. I was nine years old. Thinking of how hard she worked for so many years prompted me to write the poem.

Channels

Turquoise Water with Diamonds

It was a beautiful, long July
I stayed in turquoise water
Counting diamonds, didn't bother
With the latest news
The coyotes descending from the hills
From burned out, barren hills
I took one into my heart
I heard his bones cracking in my chest
With my every movement as I swam in the pool
I heard some time ago that the world
Soon will come to end, so I thought:
Just let me call the guy who picks up metal
Let him take the broken exercise machine

I still have this summer, watching ninja movies
Calling few friends, Andrew said: "I need
Another poem from you for the reading"
I jumped into the turquoise water again:
Looked at the sky, didn't wake up
The coyote this time, let him rest…
Others came down from the hills
One by one…. Quietly, sat by the water with diamonds
Those friends I cared about

Anna Gajewska
North Hills, CA

I am an artist, painter, and writer. I am a participant of prestigious domestic and international art exhibitions ("New American Talent" at Laguna Gloria Museum in Austin, TX; Joan Miro Drawing Exhibitions in Barcelona, Spain) as well as individual shows (Cal Poly Pomona University). "Writing helps me to express some intimate feelings better than painting, feeling like the deep concern I feel thinking of nature and all that is struggling to survive in these present times."

Across the Way

Emotions Can

All I can do is sit and guess
Why you feel such emotional distress.

Able to feel, grow, even change,
Shows everything that shouldn't remain.

Your conscience gives a sense of satisfaction
That what you are moving toward the right direction.

Visions in the night hold no clue or even what it means,
Gives you the decision to just follow your dreams.

Kimberly D. Finney
Columbus, GA

This poem is about all the sleepless nights a single mother endures over teenage children—all those nights you spend running through your mind wondering what you could have done better. It is dedicated to Alannah and Christian Finney—my reasons for being. A special thanks to Jere Smith for helping me with all those sleepless nights.

Road Show

Solitary summer walks cannot be alone
When wildflowers quietly accompany you,
As tiger-striped butterflies flap on tar and stone
Along daisy-dotted roadside within my view.

Purple, white and yellow blossoms dance in the breeze.
Button-shaped buttercups, budding lavender spears
Silently perform before my eyes—just to please.
A hidden stream concerto gurgles in my ears.

Whistling winds harmonize within bushes and trees.
Rhythmic water symphony plays to sandy shore.
Stunning blooms' dressing rooms buzz nature's "make-up" bees.
My footsteps do echo: "Bravo! Encore! Encore!"

Applaud entertainment beside the path today,
My moving premier ticket seats—center, front row.
Darting dragonflies usher me without delay
To matinee variety—a "floor-all" show!

Mary Anne Shay
Conneaut Lake, PA

Daily walk-appreciation during a 2004 Miner's Bay, Ontario vacation inspired "Road Show" and final acceptance of my Parkinson's diagnosis three years beforehand. Necessary exercise had become secondary to a late-blooming, energy-consuming teaching career. Now nature's entertaining, sensually beautiful antics amazed me as I effortlessly put words on paper. I resolved to follow the PD motto: I may have PD, but PD does not have me. A dear friend simply but wisely stated, "This is my life!" Grateful for one loving forty-year husband; two understanding children and their families; my remarkable parents; fourteen younger, supportive siblings; many friends; and God my creator.

Across the Way

Freedom

Freedom is a feeling
You keep inside your heart.
If you hold on tight to it,
You've won before the start.

For freedom is a feeling
Tested every day.
Adversaries surround us
And try to change our ways.

Because freedom is a feeling
Procured through hero's hell.
Many men gave their lives
So we could live so well.

For freedom is a feeling
No one can steal away.
The harder that they strive for it,
The stronger you will stay.

For freedom is a feeling
You can never lose.
Those feelings that you hold inside
To keep away the blues.

So take some courage from these words
And know that if you're smart,
Freedom is something you can never lose,
You keep it in your heart!

William C. Brown
Kissimmee, FL

As an American (born and bred) I feel that most of us take our freedoms for granted! We often forget that there are many countries that do not enjoy the freedoms we enjoy here. I penned this poem to help each and every one of us to remember our freedoms and to cherish them while we still have them, because over the past few years, our government officials have forgotten the basis of our rights and freedoms of "for the people by the people." Not by the government to the people. Please take a moment and remember this each and every one of us!

Bitter-Sweet Fight for Survival

The feel of the morning is cruel and unkind, the air crisp, I force myself to trek through this icy path; I find it difficult to breathe, I am struggling. My hands are in pain for the blood flows cold with the harshness of the weather, making it difficult to fulfill my journey. I cry out but no one hears me, the internal brawl with an underlying weakness has me fighting to keep control; my drive to finish what I started has me spinning.

This continuous battle is wearing but at my weakest moment, there is an overwhelming
strength that fills my soul and pulls me forward. I know not of its nature, I want to relinquish and find solace in the winter's den for it is well needed. The animal rages inside of me, I try to contain the beast but it is strong, his fight to escape sickens my mere existence. The melee between the calm and wicked is difficult, I call upon the energy and it is there, I feel as if there is nothing I cannot do.

I pay no heed to my enemies within; a dungeness cave I fall prey to. Life is whole
again, the rumble of the beast is quiet. Soothing spirits fill my being; and the course of
my journey continues. Peaceful feelings surround me guarding my emotions; a hush comes upon the room.
Until we meet again oh enemy of mine.

Dana Jackson
Angels Camp, CA

Across the Way

Things Have Changed

My dear forefathers, how things have changed.
Your Preamble, Constitution, and Amendments profaned.
Your intentions were to protect and insure freedom to all men
A system to serve the people, a jurisdiction for the innocent to defend.
It's all turned around today, inside out, upside down.
The Bible was to be reverenced, but now it's cast out.

People are now to serve these governing men,
they who distort, lie, and self-serve.
Good is called evil and evil good. Let's silence them who love God.
We will force them to worship us, "the pervert."

America was conceived upon God's laws.
Countries who ignore God will fail and descend.
They don't have God's favor and protection at all.
We see how history reveals it time and time again.

America will see God's anger with them. Don't take His wrath lightly,
He's powerful. He's Great!
He warns—consequences are coming! You're carving your tombs.
God says, "That's how it is"—there is no debate.

Take warning and heed it, you'll regret casting out God.
We'll belong to China, or who knows who we'll be.
That's where we're going. Stop now, wake up and rise.
Bring God back into our lives. He's our answer, you'll see.

Check it out, get wisdom, don't go with the flow.
Research it, don't be a clone of the trend.
Ask yourself now—"what is life's real purpose?"
The truth is, God is the Beginning and the End!

Marie Hochhalter
Pocatello, ID

Why I Should Be Thankful

Why I should be thankful,
  So many reasons why,

For taste, for touch, for thought and voice,
  A chance to see the sky.

For friends and family that I hold dear,
  A pastor that I love to hear.

For clothes, a house, and food and drink,
  Running water, heat and sink.

A language that I understand,
  The fairest laws set in the land.

A Bible I can always read,
  Salvation through which I've been freed.

Protection from the winter cold,
  An education, good as gold.

The Master's light to guide my way,
  A country where I'll have a say.

That I'm not forced into the ranks,
  And a day where I give thanks.

Although I know I'm truly flawed,
  I have a day to thank my God.

Justin Foglietta
Turner, ME

My name is Justin Foglietta, I'm fifteen years old, and I live in Turner, ME with my parents, my younger brother, my german shepherd, and a coop full of chickens. I attend Calvary Christian Academy in Turner and plan on joining the Air Force. What inspired my poem was the idea and the belief that God should be praised, not only on Thanksgiving, but every day. God has certainly blessed my family and myself. Besides poetry, I also enjoy studying military history, riding my bike, and karate.

Across the Way

Everybody Has...

Everybody has a mother
Everybody has a mother and a father
Some may know their mothers
for a lifetime —
Others a brief moment
It's not that you're not loved
because your mother is not
with you
Your mother took a detour
which didn't include you
Don't cry — strive to survive
Look to the depths for strength.
Your memory may be slight.
That certain scent, or how her
hair hung in your face making
you squint. But remember —
Everybody has a mother
Everybody has a mother and a father too
'Cause without them —
there wouldn't be you!

Sharon L. Gray
Brooklyn, NY

The Traveler

Time was spent on a dusty road,
  winds were blowing loud and bold.
Every step drew me closer to home,
  from my journey I did rome.
Things were taught and things were learned,
  growing up how my soul did yearn.
Different culture, people and places,
  contented hearts but saddened faces.
Life was simple, life was carefree,
  no one to worry about, but only me.
Clickaty clack of donkey's hoofs,
  women working, men thatching roots.
I walked with children, I walked with men,
  hearts grew fond and became good friends.
Sun beat down on golden skin,
  Cooled by breezes from northern wind.
Days go by that turn into years,
  happy contented with no fears.
Life was simple, love was true,
  living for God and not for you.

Kathy Braswell
Maylene, AL

My name is Kathy Braswell. I was born and live in Alabama. I have two grown children and four grandchildren. My family is my life, and I love them to the fullest. I enjoy crocheting, cake decorating, painting pictures and writing poetry. I draw a portion of my inspiration from my belief and love for God and my family. I write a lot of contemporary Christian poems on life, love and salvation. This poem was inspired about travel, their adventures, what they saw and people they met, but never forgetting about home.

Across the Way

My Lunar Escape

Gentle glowing moon
Draws me across my mindscape,
Bringing peace to my existence,
Acceptance of who I am.
And who I will become.
Radiant glowing light
Calms the raging mental storms.
Ominous clouds dissipate,
Allowing me to see my reflection
In the tranquil waters of my mind.
Seeing who I really am
Not who others perceive me to be.
You are my lunar utopia
Allowing me to break free.

Kathi Feldman
Seneca Falls, NY

Dragonfly

Today I see you dragonfly,
   dart here, dart there,
swoop to the sky.
Then you're gone again,
   to my chagrin.
I can't see you anymore.

Suddenly, you're up
   in front of my face!
With anxious eye,
   I follow your trace,
an ancient warrior
   commanding the sky.

You've stolen my heart
   you tiny thing.
So beautiful you are
   of color and wing.
You fascinate me, tease me,
   startle and please me.
Would I have enjoyed this walk so much
   without you?

Renée Lessert
Springfield, OR

Across the Way

Too Late

I saw him from across the room;
He turned and looked at me.
We met, we talked, but we were just
As different as could be.

We didn't care; we fell in love.
We became as one.
Who thinks about the rules of life,
When having so much fun?

But time goes on, the newness ends;
Lives somehow come apart.
Why such pain and sadness
From the boy who stole my heart?

I left; he cried; and then we went
Each our separate ways.
The minutes turned to hours,
The hours into days.

When days had turned to years
I found a hole within my heart.
I went in search of my first love,
In hope of a fresh start.

Staring in the silence
At his name upon the stone,
The love, the tears, the emptiness
Are mine and mine alone.

Toni O'Kennon Shumate
North Chesterfield, VA

valentine epitaph

she lays there in a bed of roses that turned to thorns instead
masquerading as the face of love, she created nightmares in her head

locked inside a heart of gold: pure, serene and giving...
a soul imprisoned by a thoughtless act—more dead to love than living

the door to love closed long ago as guilt became a beast
forbidding entry to a heart struggling to be released

a drowning victim gets one last breath before her death appears
she gulps it in and fades away as her heart dissolves and disappears

a 1000 fathoms underground intimacy lies buried away
among the parasites of life who use it as their prey

it's sad to think what could have been when two hearts begin to rhyme
but life's fears attack relentlessly, destroying everything sublime

epilogue:

"here lies the love of ages, ripped apart, dead-on-the-vine
decomposed and hidden from view: a valentine that was never mine"

Larry Link
Van Nuys, CA

Across the Way

A Hill in Tuscany

On a green hill beneath a brilliant Tuscan sun,
Trees, tall and straight reach to the sky,
Under their protective branches lie
Tales of men who won a war, but lost their lives.
Their dreams, desires, death stole in a flash.
Never knowing what they could have become,
On foreign soil, so far from home,
Boys one moment, then frozen in time,
Robbed of their youth, shot, left alone,
On a blood-soaked field they fought, then died.
If wars were fought by the withered old or those with pockets lined in gold,
How quickly battles would be lost and won.
The old have no time or strength for the plight so they sacrifice youth to wage their fight.
War steals the young to save the old…
That is the reason so many fought and died,
Now lying forever beneath this Tuscan sky.
During summer and autumn of '44 north of Rome,
Intense fighting scarred the hills leaving mangled dead.
Why did they have to die? Why them?
Certainly, it was not their purpose to perish,
These brave souls whose lives should be cherished.
So on a quiet knoll amidst flags swaying in a breeze,
A final resting place, so tranquil and at peace,
4,402 soldiers lie under a cerulean Tuscan sky.

Illene G. Powell
Myrtle Beach, SC

Mr. Mischief

Grandpa introduced him to it
Grandma said no, no, no
Now he cannot live without it
Uses whatever means to get it
Opens, takes, closes, hides and eats
Swears not him when caught in the act
Yes, Snuffles, you are guilty.

Runs, jumps, scratches, sniffs, pokes
Waiting patiently for the chance
To look for the forbidden introduction
Up he springs on the table, the counter
Pushes, pokes, licks, lashes with tail
With satisfied eyes swears not him
Yes, Snuffles, you are guilty.

Long and graceful, goes wherever he wills
Intimately knows every nook and cranny
Thinks he is the king and everything belongs to him
Knocks things down and could not care less
Rips and scratches what he does not like
When asked why, swears not him
Yes, Snuffles, you are guilty.

Maureen M. Evelyn
Brooklyn, NY

Across the Way

Dream

Dream of what you want to be,
no matter who tells you otherwise.
Follow the one who inspires you,
believe in yourself and you will rise.

Try again if you have no success,
you can't give up and have someone else do the rest.
Picture your life when your dream comes true,
and inspire other people as that picture becomes you.

Dajani Blagburn
Sumter, SC

Heavenly Butterfly

In all of my sorrow, sadness and pain,
My mother's spirit has shined through like the sun after the rain.

A voice deep within whispered, "You're not alone."
God has sent me to you for the love you have shown.

For now, I am a white butterfly
as you have seen!

An angel from Heaven, fluttering her wings.
Thank you God for sending my mother to me!

Carol M. Simini
Niles, OH

My Heart Knows

You grabbed my hand and said let's dance through the jungle, let's swim through the storm and carry our heavy burdens over the mountains.

You grabbed my head and said let's make way for your future amount to your dreams you are a trooper.

You grabbed my hand and put the pen to the paper, my mind has just become numb to what was once known to be a vulnerable artillery, don't mistake any of my words for speaking hypothetically, I'm speaking on reality, I confided in my mind because my heart told me, take one step at a time.

You grabbed my hand and said checkmate, I am your soul and in every weakened moment, remember I never let go.

I grabbed my soul and said thank You, God, only my heart knows.

India Green
Brooklyn, NY

Someone once told me if you don't put your talent to use the same way God gave it He'll take it. I want my words to lead people's hearts to freedom, like Harriet Tubman. I want to be heard like surround sound, create a movement like Rosa Parks when all she wanted was to sit down. Or are they trying to kill my dream like Dr. King because our dreams are better than reality? I want to be like Sojourner voicing nothing but the truth. So I decided to rise above the occasion by putting my blessing on these pages.

Across the Way

Wasted Time

We all know how to waste time,
But know not how to spend our last dime.
We need to take time to think,
Because time will be gone in a blink!

You stick your nose in a book,
And don't even take time to look
At the world all around,
Or to hear every sound,
Your desires continually abound!

Video games, TVs, and computers,
May be helpful or fun, but they're muters.
They take away conversation,
And change what we call relaxation!

We do what we want with such haste,
And don't realize how much time we waste,
Not considering others,
Our sisters and brothers,
Our neighbors, our friends, nor our mothers.

Well, there *is* still time if you care.
Yes, there *is* still time if you'll share
The love that God gave
When His Son came to save,
Then your road, He'll help you pave.

So let's all agree to bow the knee,
And let Him fill our lives and not *"me!"*

Karen Cresto
Apple Valley, CA

My poems are inspired by watching life around me. The purpose of my poems is to share feelings and encourage others to consider the important things in life, set priorities, and care about others. God first, then others, then you.

Words, Choices, Doors

I saw the other open door
where shining yellow light streams
sunflower bright light, beckoning me
and this light is joyful… for..

there are words written on flower petals
and dangling from the trees and
zinging by as shooting stars while
some recline on slow-moving clouds
and others,
like banners on birds' wings, dip and soar
still, others just endure,
as though carved on ancient rock
and a star-spangled stream flows over them
softening their angles

and they wait for me

Mary D'Aiutolo
Columbia, MD

Across the Way

My Fallen Star

I searched the heavens
dark and cold
and found a brilliance
with warmth untold.

Then down it fell…
a falling star,
to land so soft…
not near, not far.

To it I ran…
my breath of steam.
And there I found
my only dream.

Its beauty gleamed
too hot to touch.
I longed to hold
it near, so much.

Then as it cooled
it's magic grew.
I called it love…
my love for you.

To you I give
my fallen star.
Hold it near…
n'er very far.

Gary L. Coates
Palestine, TX

Moon Song

It felt as if the heavens
Had kissed the earth anew.
Clouds gently rocked the mountains,
New flowers would accrue.
The sun began to wander
Around the hidden world.
To keep her from a blunder,
Moon came and unfurled
Night with soothing dew,
So Sun would not burn plants so new.
The stars now felt abandoned
As they had naught to do.
So Moon said, "Come my little children
And light the way for me.
We'll make a good assembly
And forever it shall be."

Jutta E. Woitscheck
Fort Pierce, FL

Writing poetry in English comes surprisingly easy to me since it was my second language. I grew up speaking German for one third of my life. Quite a bit different stylistically. "Moon Song" was inspired by me watching the stars and moon from my balcony at night when sleep eludes me, as happens to many elderly people. I wrote it for my, at the time, young granddaughter. By now I have composed enough poems to have them published in a book of my own. I'd like to become the "Grandma Moses of Poetry" before I climb the crystal ladder to the stars.

Life

We should all enjoy life to the fullest each new day
Always give thanks to God above and don't forget to pray
Without Him, there would be no trees
animals, sun, earth or you and me
Whether you are happy or sad, time
flies by so very quickly
Life is way too short to sit back
and waste, so I won't waste mine
To be called to Heaven above
Only God knows when it's your time
It's always a plus in life to lend a
helping hand to someone in need
Whether you give your time, patience,
love or to the hungry you feed
Life can be so full of happiness, friends
family and maybe even true romance
You will never know unless you listen
to your heart and take a chance
I know life does come with many
tough ups and downs
But they'll be easier to deal with
just as long as you have loved
ones around

Savalya Robinson
Orlando, FL

I was born and raised in Queens, NY. I come from a large family. I have five sisters and only one brother. I'm bi-racial and also a Christian. I'm an animal lover, but cats have always been my first true love. I enjoy taking pictures, writing poetry, playing word games, and before I injured my back I also enjoyed bowling, shooting pool, dancing, and horseback riding. I'm a single mother of four and I've been blessed with seven grandchildren. Many situations in life inspired me to write this poem, which took me only forty-five minutes to create from my heart.

I Am

I am a girl who loves to swim.
I wonder if mermaids exist.
I hear the crashing waves in the sea.
I see cool plants and creatures.
I want to be a mermaid under the sea.
I am a girl who loves to swim.

I pretend to be a mermaid.
I feel the tiny bubbles popping on my face.
I touch the amazing plants.
I worry that I'll get eaten.
I cry when someone passes away.
I am a girl who loves to swim.

I understand that we all can't live forever.
I say have a great life on land and sea.
I dream that mermaids are real.
I try to be the best swimmer ever.
I hope they do find that mermaids exist.
I am a girl who loves to swim.

Melissa M. Torres
El Paso, TX

Across the Way

Practice Will Make Par-fect

My heart pounded in rhythm with my steps as I approached the tee box. I bent and pierced the tough ground with my tee, then gently placed the ball atop.

I stood and steadied myself, took a deep breath, inhaling the earthy scent of the freshly mowed fairways. I was poised and ready to strike, focusing intently on that little white, dimpled object so casually called a ball.

Had I swallowed sand? My lips and mouth were so parched and dry. I purposefully wrapped my palm around my club, feeling the ridges of the grip press into my skin. Slowly I twisted back, club high in the air. And then, the sudden uncoiling like a giant spring.

Contact. The clink of the club striking the ball, sounding like a crisp head of lettuce being ripped apart, the echo ringing in my ears as I watched the little white sphere soar higher and further away from me.

Traveling its invisible arc in the sky until I could barely make it out. Lazily slumping into the soft sand directly in front of the lush green, holding the flag, tauntingly waving at me.

You missed!

Beth A. Romano
Fitchburg, MA

Where Am I?

In a place of stone and sand,
Come travelers to rest and drink.

Scooping up water by hand
To refresh oneself, to ponder and think.

No need to guard, sit or stand,
Sleep while you can 'cause camels stink.

Dunes are high, mystic and grand,
Walk as if in snow or you'll sink.

Skies of blue, nothing around only land,
It's in eye's view, so please don't blink.

To wonder or guess where am I and
If you have, I'll smile and wink!

Marjory Trigili
Las Vegas, NV

Across the Way

Daddy's Girl

Does it make you cringe when I talk about the men you're not
The people you can never be and the parts of me you have never
    seen
The guts and glory that make me up, that fill me... that make me
    real?

Don't you know you helped put them there?
You've seen them in their growing stages
Touched the darkest recesses and strove to bring them light

From you I have grown even in the distance
The challenges you demand no straight answers
A guiding shot in the dark with wobbly brakes

You shove and make me find my wings
Never far behind the mix of joy and pain your eyes
Crossing your fingers not holding your breath

I sink and rise and rise and fall again
The steady-handed bicycle just after you let go
The tears in your throat the song in your eyes

I know

Lisa L. Gibson
Aurora, CO

Mom

You remember, Mom, on the day I was born,
You wrapped me up in your arms to keep me warm.
   Looking back at this little girl that was here,
you knew, Mom, there was nothing to fear.
   Tiny hands and little feet that melted
your heart with a skip of a beat.
   A tiny treasure that you adored, with
all your heart you couldn't love me more.
   The little girl, then a young women as I
grew up to be, a gift of life, there's nothing
more but the best was yet to be.
   You remember, Mom, of all the years gone by,
Dad, sister too, times as a family with
grandkids too.
   Thank you, Mom, as I will always
remember you, you're an angel now and a
whisper in the wind, I'll remember you,
Mom, as the day closes in.

Lorraine Orsinger
Irwin, PA

To start with, first and foremost I love writing poems. I've always been a creative person. I also do photography. I'm also married and a mom to two girls, and I love every minute of it. My mother was a source of inspiration. I'll always remember all of the fun times with her, my dad and older sister as a family. So with my pen in hand and paper, all the words in my poem are from the heart and my deepest soul. May you rest in peace, Mom. This poem is for you. I love you.

Across the Way

Any Day Is Mother's Day

A beautiful act took place today —
An act of love along life's way.
My young son, with love in his eyes,
Came in and said "Mom, I have a 'supwise'!"

How could I guess what it might be,
As he hid it behind him and said to me,
"Now 'cwose' your eyes an' hold out your han'."
So I did so, for he's a sweet young man.

He handed to me a little bouquet —
Yard weeds they were, but on *this* day
No roses or orchids could ever be
Any more lovely than yard weeds to me!

Joy L. King
Bivins, TX

Oceans Away

Fly on:
   With majesty you wave the standard
   High above ships sinking at sea
   Tattered jack of red and blue on white
   Truly you fly, forever free
   Carry me home like a soldier in his flag
   Your price is a heavy one to pay
   Pine boxes in a masque of velvet stars and stripes
   Oh Lord, I'm oceans away

Shine on:
   In darkness you shine—a ray of hope
   Over garrisons awake, involved in the fight
   The torch you hold is now in my hands
   (Be soothed by Mother Liberty's light)
   Guide me home like a soldier in glory
   The price of death paid heavily today
   Cities erupt in brilliance and are gone
   Oh Lord, give me an ocean to sail away

Ring on:
   In victory you ring liberty's noise
   The sound is heard throughout the land
   The pealing timbre is cracked with emotion
   Behold—freedom's mighty hand
   Yet you brought me home a soldier in sorrow
   I had no idea I would pay this way
   Church bells ring forever in memory
   Oh Lord, I'm still oceans away

Jill D. Gerlach
Kingsport, TN

Across the Way

Sharing

We share the clouds, we share the sun,
We share the sadness, and we share fun.
We share the sky, we share the stars,
The worlds shared no matter who you are.

We share hate, we share love,
Just do me a favor, and look above.
Because in this world, there's *One* who cares,
And *God's* that person whom we all share.

Patricia M. Madigan
Penn Yan, NY

Katrina, Katrina

Water and wind depressed the night
Taking the shaft of nature's plight
Breaking boundaries and boundless waves
Setting its right to making graves.
Katrina, Katrina no doubt you've heard
Its fate, its destiny can be observed
Destructive patterns with its restlessness
Towards mankind is filled with hopelessness
Oh how hopeless, oh how heartless it can be
Devouring what's in its path and spreading debris
Katrina, Katrina to your life I confess
Katrina, Katrina, you're just a putrid mess.

Tibor T. Kexcon
Desert Hot Springs, CA

My Darling Bud

The first gift you gave me lies there on the dresser,
a small lovely heart on a chain.
The card read, "To the Love of My Life."
My feelings for you were the same.

For you truly were the love of my life
with a heart so sweet and true.
Your love lifted me to unbelievable heights
You said my love did the same for you.

Oh how rich and deep was our love,
total trust and such sweet harmony.
Like a magnet, we were drawn to each other,
like streams of water rushing into the sea.

The powerful current of our love swept us on
as deeper and deeper we plunged,
until we were completely immersed
and our two hearts did indeed beat as one.

Alma L. Swink-Jones
Woodland, CA

Across the Way

My Silent Heart

Sometimes I want to write a poem,
When I really have nothing to say,
In spite of hopes and dreams galore,
Or the burdens of the day.

I sit and stare for hours
At a paper white as snow.
But what to write upon it,
My mind just doesn't know.

My heart could tell me if it would,
Just what it wants to speak.
The words unheard by mortal ears,
The strong, the rich, the weak.

Beyond the secret doors are hid
The words I have not spoken,
The words that hide in silence now,
For the doors I could not open.

Donna G. Simpson
Crofton, KY

Our Grandkids

There is nothing like a grandchild
to make you feel your worth.
Whenever you first see them,
the feeling you have is like no other on Earth.

Grandkids are a gift from God,
there is absolutely no doubt.
You feel so sensational
You just want to scream and shout!

Our grandchildren are so very great!
And they make us so, so proud.
Oh how entertaining they can be.
And can always pick you out in a crowd.

You watch them grow up way too fast,
they're full of love so good and true.
So sincere and so funny also;
And amazing how much they love you!

So love your grandchildren with all your heart,
Giving them all you have to give.
Help them to always stay on the right path and
Just love them dearly for as long as you live!

Patti Howell
Luray, TN

Across the Way

The Light Remains

I found the light, or the light found me.
And it hurt to know just what He'd see
was me.

  'Cause what I saw,
He saw,
They all saw
Me fall
To my knees.

  With loving hand rested on my head,
He said, drink this instead.
And I opened my eyes to see the red
of His blood.

  With that, He washed away all my sin
And said, blood washed you begin
A new life.

  What you've been given is free,
Because I hung on that tree,
And gave all.

  There will be many a day
When you doubt what I say,
But hold fast.
  I've washed all your stain.
Don't hold on to your pain.
  I remain.

Michael S. McClellen
Parker, KS

Destiny of an Educator

Life is short and life is slow
At early ages most don't know where they'll go
Some go near and some go far
As for myself I am reaching for a star
I don't make much if measured in gold
But I am getting wealthy as I grow old
I am perfectly content to be just sowing seeds
As I serve America's educational needs

When former students come back and tell me
Where they have been
It makes me know I would do it all over again
Sometimes it gets weary along the way
But I just get ready for another school day

Roy V. Davis
Durant, OK

Across the Way

I Am Who I Have Come to Be

Am I who I have come to be?

I live with a bunch of people but yet I still feel lonely
I love, I hate, I never hold a grudge
I stand 10 feet tall just to be knocked down 5 feet shorter

I withhold or hide what's really inside
I don't let you in and when I do
I end up showing you the past rage from above

I hope and pray and wonder
Is my future what I want or assume it to be?
Because I am who I have come to be.

Or am I honestly a man and woman's mistake
That time caught up with?
Am I a letdown to society?

Am I really who I have come to be?
I am child of the wrong and confusion
I am what my past or ancestors want me to be.

Am I who I have come to be?

Vernessa Caldwell
Hollandale, MS

Hi, my name is Vernessa Caldwell. I am sixteen years old. I am the third child out of four. My mother's name is Camisa Caldwell; she is a single parent. She's the glue that sticks all of us together. I have an older sister and brother and a younger sister. My life at times is crazy. That's why I wrote the poem "I Am Who I Have Come to Be." It was an expression of how I felt. At times it's like I am in a fairy tale and then I am in a nightmare. I sometimes fear that my past will interfere with my future, because where I am from, the struggle is real!

Homeless

Sitting down in the cold
just her mother to hold
Ripped blankets and a box
greasy brown locks
Pale white skin
small old bin
Some money they ask
people walk by fast
Innocence in the eyes
but people think just lies
Thin purple lips
skinny thin hips
No way home
lost and alone
Ripped up shoes
singing the blues
Hungry and thirsty
begging for mercy
In need of a home
stuck in a dome
Nowhere to go
minds working slow
Mother and daughter
A pig to the slaughter

Erika M. Galeczka
Hainesville, IL

Across the Way

Release

My head is spinning, tumbling, turning.
In my heart there is a yearning
And my body feels a burning
Want for something, what I do not know.
But I feel that I lay wasted.
Innumerable challenges lay untasted.
My experience is pictures, pasted
Up by those who do and see and go.
What I want is fire, thunder,
Something to pull my thoughts asunder,
Something to get me out from under
These mournful thoughts that oppressively flow.
Put me on a cloud, a carriage;
Give me an outer life, a marriage
With something I cannot disparage,
To give me room to roam, or stay, but grow.

Lenore Phyle
Marion, MT

The Flying Opossum

It was half past eight and I was running late.
So down the steps I flew, only thinking of you.
With one step to go, before my eyes I see,
this opossum jumps out in front of me.
He raised up, bared his teeth and grinned,
then let out a screech that stood my hair on end.
I couldn't help it, I was in mid-stride,
as I drop-kicked that opossum right over the Shop-N-Ride!
Not believing what just happened, I didn't miss a beat.
I jogged over to the store across the street.
Ole Norm worked nights at the store you see,
and he had stepped out for a smoke and some breeze.
As I rounded the corner I said, "Hey Norm, What's up?"
He looked at me kind of star struck and mumbled "Uhhhh."
"You ain't gonna believe this, but I swear it's no lie.
That there opossum just fell out of the sky!"
He took a long drag from his smoke and replied,
"It just fell from the sky. I tell you it's true.
Down it came from right out of the blue!"
As he stood there scratching his head in wonder,
I thought it best to confess my blunder.
I told ole Norm what happened from beginning to end.
We laughed till we cried, we'd stop and start again.
As he took a last drag from his smoke he replied,
"Let's just keep this between us if you don't mind.
'Cause I'd never live it down the night I saw opossum fly!

Julee Lemons
Loudon, TN

Across the Way

Reverie

Along a path comes winding
with winter winds that blow
a crest-fallen maiden waits
by the road, on the hill, in the snow

Her frosty glance speaks volumes
crystal sets her tearful eyes
with heartfelt icy-breath emotion
through a gale of wind, she sighs

Stirring a girlish longing there
for an unfrozen vine
on sunny limbs that sway
tender feelings, so sublime

She's a white-shrouded lady
who's yearning to be free
to fling her cloak of winter
against a budding tree

Daydreams of a flowery branch
the warm kiss of spring
a verdant path, a sanctuary
and every other lovely thing

So casts a glowing reflection
in a mirror that winters made
awakens a springtime reverie
by the sea, on the meadow, in the glade

Laurie Plymale
Carlisle, PA

I have always been interested in poetry and as a child, I loved the rhymes with musical feelings. As a lover of nature I often combine the two. Having vivid dreams throughout the years, I often hear poetry or see landscapes, which inspire me. Sitting quietly too, just listening to the pulse of nature, brings me peace. In that stillness, I feel the spiritual energy they bring. Call it love or God, inspiration or peace, it all feels the same to me.

The Crate

I crated up my wisdom to give it all away
Because I really wasn't sure I'd see another day.
'Twas knowledge freely given and so I'll freely give
A higher form of life and a better way to live.
Methought, my children are the first I want to give it to,
But then they claimed the things I had they already knew.
And what I knew, said they, had come from all the ages past;
And I, they said, should surely know that old stuff doesn't last.
So then I took my crate to town to wisen up that lot,
But many told me univers'ties where they had been taught
The right for wrong and wrong for right—professor's usual course.
They're teaching all their students to become a new-world force.
I took it to the politicians, lawyers and then more—
The leaders of the world all saw the crate when out on tour,
But all they really cared about was how opponents felt
And would they lose their power if opinion starts to tilt.
Discouraged thrice, I did not know what else that I could do
And so I put away my crate with all the wisdom, too.
And many years went by until the day I fin'lly died—
The earth at peace and full of love for all those years denied.
And generations came and went until a young lad found
The crate with all the wisdom—then cried with such a sound,
"With all the wisdom here employed we could have had world peace
And love enough for ev'ryone—a love that couldn't cease."

John E. Sherman
Baytown, TX

Across the Way

A Mother Is a Treasure

A gift from God, that exceeds diamonds
And pearls, each day a mother's love is
Fresh like the morning dew…
A mother's heart is delicate like a rose
petal, a mother's heart bears all things,
trusts all things, a mother's love is precious
A reflection of God's unconditional love…
A mother is always asking for God's wisdom
Through understanding with a hearing heart
With a humble heart to listen and understand
God's heart through a mother's heart
of love…

Gloria Candelaria
Rio Rancho, NM

I dedicate this poem to my son Paul, you are very special to me. You are my inspiration and joy, you hold a special place in my heart. Thank you for the encouragement. I love you. I also dedicate this poem to my mother, Frances, in her honor for her strength and determination in raising fourteen children on her own, with love—our dad died of illness. We thank this awesome woman for keeping us all together as a family. We thank God for this beautiful mother, who is our treasure.

I Love You More

I love you more than french fries
Awash with chili cheese
Pickle chips and chicken strips
I love you more than these.

More than soft ice cream or pizza
Or coconut cream pie
Peanut butter cookies
Or the blue in summer's sky.

More than blackened popcorn
Or ripe tomatoes from the vine
The sight and scent of laundry
Dancing on the line.

More than Charleston and gardens
And the mighty ocean's roar
A gentle breeze, autumn leaves
A screen on my back door.

More than rabbits or gorillas
Or puppies by the score
Lilac trees or dragonflies
Oh, I love you so much more.

Than reading in a cozy nook,
Wading in a quiet brook,
A spot of shade, a lemonade,
Pictures from the past,
Birds that sing, a front porch swing
I love you more than anything.

Janice M. Anteau
Monroe, MI

Across the Way

The Knight of Vengeance

There was once a white knight
Who fended evil on sight
With white, polished steel
With qualities our ideal

His thoughts are bright, bleached in light
Sword in hand to fight, this being set his height

Where light shines, a shadow is cast
The white knight had a vapid past
The darkness brought him down so low
It manifested into a crow

The coal black crow, perched on his pauldron
Its dirty talons stain the soul
Corruption seeps in the white armor cauldron
With the darkness difficult to control

A dame fair, love and lust pair
To ensnare, the knight didn't care

Under a face he trusts
Brash action bled, his depression rose
The knight's armor rusts
Armor pieces shed, his heart exposed

Leapt the crow, its talons dug deep
The fatal blow, his soul ready to reap

A soul once pure, stained with conviction
There is no cure from blind addiction
The knight believed in his purity
His sword grieved from reckless insecurity

Benjamin Z. Craig
Ashland, PA

Passion

My passion for nature grew and grew
Till I became a part of it, too;
Now I see the seasons come and go
And watch the tides ebb and flow.

When I breathe
A breeze begins stirring,
And when I sing
The birds start chirping;
When I'm sick
The world is gloomy and gray,
But when I laugh
The earth turns sunny and gay.

With my paintbrush
I can paint the ground,
Or flowers, or sunsets,
Or leaves all around;
I care for the land, the water,
And ev'ry creature;
This is why
I am called Mother Nature.

Elizabeth Anderson
Frederick, MD

Across the Way

A New Moon Day

The sky will darken
as white ice falls
We so feel this new
Season when winter
calls

A falling snow to
cover the ground
as the night wolves
scurry
They're hard to be
found

The sun is restless
to reappear
It shall return
We have no fear

And so as the cold
winds begin to fade
away

We wait upon
A New Moon Day

Karen M. LoCicero
Mt. Pleasant, SC

Eternal Devotion

Today you were taken away.
Oh so far, won't see you every day.
I cared for and helped you in every way.
Never asking for a promotion,
My love is a symbol of everlasting devotion.
We had great times,
Some not so great in between,
So thankful I have God's shoulder on which to lean.
I ask God to fill me with peace in my heart
For our love can endure even though we're apart.
In my heart, for you there will always be a place.
I will carry my memories and always your sweet face.
I know you love me and want me to rest,
I'll catch up with family and enjoy life at its best.
Today you were taken away!
But until the end of this life
I will always be your wife.

Gail Waltman
Santee, CA

A poem to reflect love and respect to my dear mother, age eighty-two, who helped my father throughout his twelve-year journey with Alzheimer's while living at home. As my father's disease moved along it became impossible for my mother to care for him. He now lives in a nursing home forty miles away. After sixty-three years of marriage it has been difficult to start a new way of living without him. She is doing her best and has support from her loving family.

Across the Way

Learning to Do Without

If we would pay when we pick up,
no credit on the sly—
if we would only purchase what
we could afford to buy;
indeed we'd have a lot more cash,
of that there is no doubt—
to have a lot, I guess you have
to learn to do without.

If we would sacrifice our wants
and minimize our needs—
if we'd quit buying flowers and
just learn to live with weeds—
no shopping, no vacations and
no costly evenings out—
our bank accounts would flourish as
we learned to do without.

Yes, either way, one does without
one thing or another—
I guess we cannot have it all,
just one or the other.
To do without possessions or
cold cash and all its clout?
I guess life's made out of the things
we learn to do without.

Janet L. Emery
Sun City, AZ

Sire of Sires

Cosmic tree extending the whole universe
   Sustaining and giving life in abundance
Untouched by birth and death has unique power
   Ever awake like a glorious blossomed flower
Protected with elegant shoulder caps, looks valiant
   Immeasurable form and prowess, is very gallant
The very vital foundation and ultimate support
   Supreme controller with none above to report
Possesses ultimate authority over all scriptures
   Provides knowledge that elevates into rapture
The supreme soul as an epitome of reality
   Truth and virtue giver as beliefs in morality
The true spirit who maintains all *His* deeds
   Like a rower moving us to sail in life needs
Embodiment of hope and accomplishing sacrifice
   Sire of *sires*, helping for righteous path to paradise

Krishna Devulapalli
Mentor, OH

Across the Way

Epilogue

Something happens on some days, something changing all our ways.
Beliefs and morals, once steadfast, are now just whimsies of the past.
All those futures that we created in our youth now seem outdated,
And the loves that once made us thrive now make us wish we weren't alive.

Something changes throughout the years, we notice rusting on the gears.
And all at once, in just a day, innocent youth has faded away.
Where did all those dreams go, can dreams just melt away like snow?
The past just seems so effervescent, so unlike the dreary present.

Sometimes fear is suffocating, and the laws of nature devastating
That with life, so pure, comes death, so secure.
Everything fades fast, and morphs into pictures of the past;
Memories that seem to glisten, all those words that I have written.

Sometimes lessons are learned too late; too long does wisdom make us wait.
This place that once made me happy now leaves me feeling empty,
Longing for days gone by, I just glance up at the sky;
Parallel to life, sunny and cloudy and shapeless, stretching to an end we can't assess.

Sometimes I write words on empty pages, though they don't bring me sage or wages,
Meaningless to all but me, still I type devotedly
To fill the empty hours ticking past, so that perhaps the words will last
And be around when I am gone, and perhaps they, at least, will carry on.

Taylor E. Redger
Arvada, CO

Santa

There's not a big chubby guy coming
down my chimney with a long
white beard, come on, you're kidding me.
There's not a man in my house in
a red jump suit.
Come on! There's not a reindeer
on my roof.

Santa's not real! Santa's not real!

He's just a fake, it's your parents'
mistake for lying to you on
Christmas Eve.

Now let's talk about that guy at
the mall... I think we all know
that his beard is not real at all!
I'm sure he's tall and very thin,
I think he just stuffs pillows
within.

Santa's not real! Santa's not real!

Santa's not real!

Sara Bailey
Redmond, OR

Sara is eight and a half years old. She is in the third grade and is homeschooled. This poem is actually a song she invented one day in anticipation of Christmas 2013. Her grandma enjoyed it so much she encouraged us to enter it in this poetry contest. As her family, we were not completely surprised because she loves to sing, dance, and create original stories, but this one was clearly and persuasively unique. Her audience needed to hear the truth! When we asked what inspired her work she simply replied, "I think it's just creepy that anyone would want a complete stranger to break into their house at Christmas."

Across the Way

Oh Weeden

In the eye of the storm oh Weeden and your crew,
The abyss calls us from the depth of the ocean floor;
It surrounds our soul with death and despair.
Our redeemer, we see you as lighting glows in the brightness of
    His eye.
His voice echoes in the darkness in the eye of thine storm,
Tear drops of pain in the garden, as tear drops of rain failing into
    the abyss.
Three days in the eye of the storm,
The raging waves surround our soul.
Take the helm and lead us home, oh Lord,
Leave us not in the eye of the raging storm.
My Lord and saviour, you answered our call.
Your Word is ever true, you carried the Weeden home ashore,
Where is home oh Weeden,
Your bell tolls no more,
Where is home.

Joe J. Espinoza
Glendale, AZ

Channels

January Grey

Grey the sky, this January day
Resolutions anew
Some will stay, while others stray
Verses express, award is found
When our passions are our ground
Differences may be seen
Find ways within our means
Pursue the dream
Some it comes easy, others such a row
Retire all too soon, by their own
Disappointment in yourself
Fearing others may reciprocate
Grey, this January day
Here comes three hundred and sixty-five days
Putting forth our best efforts
If we chose to pursue higher
We may start constructing our staircase
Environment encases many unknowns
Our base may sway
An alley here, a pathway there
Some may warn Dead End
Taking knowledge we've consumed
Other routes come into view
We will ensue
Amelioration of our hue

Jana Woods
Rock Springs, WY

Across the Way

Nicotine

There are a thousand whispered words in the hazy smoke
that laces its way around us, weaving its breath into our throats.

I watch the cigarette that dangles between your ever-present smirk,
threatening to turn my focused thoughts into a messy cloud of you.

The nicotine that coats your lungs fuels your need
for self-destruction.

I would tell you that all I can do is watch while my helpless tongue
lies flat, begging to tell you everything.

If my chest didn't stir every time your mouth curled up, I would
tell you that your hands shake when they brush your cigarette box.

If I didn't feel my veins spark alive whenever your mocha eyes
find mine, I would tell you that the answer that you search for
at the bottom of every bottle will never appear.

If I didn't have sleepless nights where you invaded my every thought,
I would tell you that the words that spill out of your lips
dance in the dreams of poets.

I inhale the smoke billowing around you instead of saying a word,
letting the toxic breath race through my insides before I blow it out,
humming the words I could never say into the haze.

The smoke curls around your ear, whispering that you are
destroying
the beautiful pieces of you.

Those pieces have finished the puzzle that flows out of my
worn notebook, with you illuminated by the dim lamplight
dripping onto the pages of my thoughts.

Your nicotine smile tells me that you'd ruin me.
Then I'm yours to ruin.

Nicole Andrasko
Moon Township, PA

Olive Branch

In your eyes,
   I see His eyes.
Captured by your gaze,
My heart is set ablaze!

You brought me near,
Destroying my fear.
Tender as a dove,
Enraptured by your love.

You came to my side,
And made me your Bride.
Standing face to face,
   I feel His grace.

I am one who has been won—

Like an Olive Branch from the
heart of Father,
is my Brother's love for me!

Joy Krista VanDeLoo
Eau Claire, WI

"Olive Branch" is very special to me because it was divinely inspired. I was awakened in the middle of the night on November 21, 2011 around 3:00 a.m., moved in my spirit to write this piece. Although this piece speaks of romance between a man and woman, it also speaks of Jesus and His Bride. He himself is the Olive Branch from Father; the extension of peace and friendship through His death and resurrection on the Cross at Calvary. He is my older brother, my bridegroom, my friend. John 3:16–17. Thank you, Mom, for telling me to do this!

Across the Way

Bear in Mind

Here a bear, there a bear, everywhere I roam;
   I have so many hunting stories, I could write a poem.
You may believe my story, as tall the tale may seem;
   Could it all be very true, or is it just a dream?
Now, I am a true hunter, how do you do?
   I like hunting bear, for my wild game stew.
I never miss, I make one shot kills;
   I'll hunt along the rivers, or up in the hills.
Hunting bear is not so easy, because they are so clever;
   If you can't outsmart them, you'll be skunked forever.
Now, look into my eyes and you will see no fear;
   That bear is in danger if he is anywhere near.
You better not miss, and that is for certain,
   Or the Bear will get his turn, and you'll come back a hurtin'.
If you run out of bullets, you better have a knife;
   'Cause getting scared and runnin' ain't going to save your life.
If you don't have success out in the woods,
   There are other methods ten times as good.
Plant some watermelon around your hunting shack;
   Sit back and relax, that bear will come back.
Strap your flashlight to your rifle, and sit out after dark,
   Guarding your watermelon, waiting for your dog to bark.
Have a little patience, and sometime in the night,
   That hungry critter will appear in the barrel of your flashlight.
What is there to brag about? Your hunt is done, and then,
   You wake up from your hunting dream, and realize... the bear has won again!

Stephen W. Hedstrom
Brighton, CO

I grew up in a small farming community in rural North Dakota. I developed a passion for hunting and fishing at a very young age. The great outdoors has continued to be an important part of my life. I am also a Vietnam veteran. Sitting many hours on riverbanks and hillsides has allowed my mind to escape from the memories of my experience in the jungles of Vietnam and life's everyday issues. The serenity of the outdoors has provided me the freedom to put my thoughts into my poetry.

April

My name is April, sir!
I often laugh, as
often cry.
I cannot tell what
makes me,
Only that the seasons
overtake me.
I must dimple, smile
and frown,
Laughing while the
tears roll down.
But that's nature, Sir!
not art,
And I'm happy for
my part.

Judy Ann Smith
Lockport, NY

Across the Way

Yes

Yes, Mr. Dunn, you may get up to 75 years.
That will never ease the hurt or dry up a mother's crying tears.

Yes, Mr. Dunn, she may have forgiven you,
but that will never change the pain or the heartache that you put her through.

Yes, there's no justice for this young man's life.
Nothing in the world will ever make it right.

Yes, they should change the law that says "Stand your ground."
If not, young black boys will continue to be shot down.

Yes, some prejudiced people think black kids are always doing wrong,
Black children are not safe wearing hoodies or playing their rap songs.

Yes I think we have come a very long way.
Will things ever be equal? I can only hope and pray.

Carolyn Brown
Edison, NJ

My name is Carolyn Hart-Brown, I am a sixty-seven-year-old mother of three wonderful children and the proud grandmother of four beautiful grandchildren. I grew up in South Carolina in the sixties. I could not wait to graduate from school and leave the south because of all the racism there. Sadly we have not moved that far from the sixties, black men are still treated harshly in this country, our jails reflect that. Now our young black men are being shot down, how sad is that? So I write about injustice, hoping for change.

Lost… and Found

When you're tested by life's trials
and you don't know where to turn,
just call out to the Savior—
He will help you His mercies to learn.

Just remember after He's rescued you
and put your feet on solid ground,
you were once, oh so needy,
you were lost and… now you're found.

When you're walking through life's valleys,
and the way seems strange and dim,
take the hand of the One who loves you—
He will lead you; He'll carry you through.

Just remember when you've come through the valley,
and He's brought you safe and sound,
you were once, oh so needy,
you were lost and… now you're found.

I was lost and… now I'm found.

Laura Seidel
Belle Rive, IL

Across the Way

From Whence Happiness Springs

Just forgive as well you should
  All hurts for your own good.
Envy not and enjoy each day;
  Avoid to get in your own way.
Serve others generously,
  And contented you will be.
Under all, always show love,
  Which comes down from up above.
Strive for patience every day,
  And things will tend to go your way.
If you're always honest and true,
  Blessings will gravitate to you.
Sow smiles and encourage always,
  For a long life and happy days.
Give your anger no room to grow,
  So you will have good health to sow.
Opt to be respectful and kind,
  Which will result in peace of mind.
Do follow each of the above,
  And in this life you'll find much love.

Linda Hodges
Discovery Bay, CA

Flower

Color of deepest hue,
   bursting with passion true.
Wine for few,
   tailored for you.
Blossoming love,
   wide-eyed blue.
Mornings awake,
   love rings true.

Patricia Nance
Lake Stevens, WA

Fools

Here I am all by myself
Though a married man I'll be
My wife is in another world
So far away from me
If I live or should I die
No matter says she
I'll just find another fool
And again, happy I'll be
The moral of this poem
My friend, is to wisely choose
Or you could be another one
Picked from the list of fools

Gene Gordon
Webster, NY

Across the Way

Goodbye, Dragonfly

That which dwells within oneself
Is all but fluttering in an updraft of downward spirals,
Enticed from oneself, and snared from whence it came,
Out from the belly of the beast,
Unsprung from a coil of heartwrenching
Breaks and fractures from its underlying
Foundation and common bonds of swept pain,
Sadness, sorrow and loss, perhaps the very loss
Of innocence once bestowed unto our savage,
Confused souls formally we inquire of its state,
Unwanting to know the real condition of our own self,
And the right of passage which we have blocked from ourselves,
Right of passage, wrongly blocked by years of manifesting and
decomposing
From the bowels of our own destruction dwelling under
Stars, moon and the sun.
And yet there is the love for and from our daughters
And mothers and fathers and brothers,
If not found, it too will be lost,
Yet again, in the farthest of our own minds,
Comes the timberlands in these we hide from ourselves
And from our fears and reality comes in after us,
But yet, who is the hunted and who is the prey?
In disbelieving and dismay we know both are
Reclaimed by our soul,
Proclaimed the same back again
The eye to the window of the soul.

Cynthia Graham-Lemon
Marysville, KS

Mom's Crooked Teeth

Pearly white and crooked too
it bites good food
that dad's freshly cooked

And mom's 26 teeth
are good fore more.

And her other teeth are nice and sharp.
Mom's teeth
are an inspiration for me and you.

Mom's are special,
special like dad.

But Father's Day is far away
so back off dad,
today is Mother's Day.

Michael S. Bedner
Chandler, AZ

My name is Michael Salomao Bedner. I was born in Port Chester, NY. My father is American and my mother is Brazilian. I have a twin sister and a younger brother. I enjoy reading and writing. When I was eight years old I wrote a lot of poems. My mom always talked about her crooked teeth and one day I'd had enough and wrote a poem to get her to pipe down. One of my biggest wishes is to write and draw a comic book. We live in Arizona now. Cheers.

Across the Way

Celebrate Maya

Some souls arrest their development,
   Consumed by self-pity and shame,
Maya obeys inner yearnings —
   Strives hard to gain fortune and fame.

She *electrifies* words, movement, speech.
   Makes bland English impact the soul.
Her birthings of unclassic creation
   Are brilliant jewels of gold.

She is both *herself* and *us* at the same time,
   Articulates our history with pride,
Realizes the depths of our struggles,
   Describes how a people survive.

Come feast at her literary bounty —
   Prose, lyrics, poetry and plays.
Listen as she weaves a story.
   Move with her rhythmic sways.

Let's embrace her wisdom and her wit,
   As she strives to reach higher heights,
Keeping firm on the pulse of the people,
   Bringing peace, love, and joy as she writes.

Saisa Neel
Annapolis, MD

Born, raised, and educated in Washington, D.C., I am a product of the African American revolutionary struggles of the 1960s. My generation was the continuation of the earlier civil rights movement and the on-going struggle for human rights for African peoples worldwide. While white youngsters were identifying themselves as "hippies" and testing the limits of the culture that their ancestors created, we were protesting the conditions that we did not create — substandard housing, poor schools, crime-filled neighborhoods, low-paying jobs, despair and hopelessness infecting the next generation. I Know Why the Caged Bird Sings, published in 1969, was my first exposure to renowned artist Maya Angelou. I came to the table late, not until 1998, and because of it became a Maya Angelou "groupie." My poem is homage to my heroine. I have been influenced by many factors in my more than six decades on this planet, all of which have filled me with satisfaction, a sense of worthiness, and heartfelt joy. However, artists like Maya Angelou lift my spirits to new heights, as they inspire me to continue the struggle.

Path of the World

We go about our daily lives without a care for the next man
Not knowing if the person sitting across from us has played a part in our
past or will in our future
We find it so easy to belittle each other, holding each other down when we
are all struggling to rise
Each person has a burden in life, everyone just carries it differently
The guy that pulls up next to us at the red light, could've just found out his
wife is terminally ill
The young lady sitting next to us, could have found out that she's
expecting but doesn't know what to do
The man we just bought our paper from business isn't doing well he could
be worrying how he's going to take care of his family
Why should we care?
Our problems are so much worse
Kindness or even simple human compassion is beneath us
We have all come from somewhere, we are all striving to go
somewhere
We can't get there the way we are today
It's time to make a change; this world is so much bigger than
individuals.

Sonya Goddard
Brooklyn, NY

Across the Way

Blessings of the Meadow

I come to the meadow when I am
Having a sad day.
Here, the wild flowers greet me
Dressed in their colors so gay.
The beautiful flowers and lovely tall trees
Are all just dancing in the gentle breeze.
The birds are chirping and singing their happy songs,
The bees are buzzing, and the beautiful butterflies
Come waltzing along.
Yesterday's memories come flooding back, my love.
I feel you are looking down from above.
God took you to your heavenly home,
And left me here all alone.
But I come to the meadow when I am blue.
All these blessings remind me of you.
We spent many happy hours
Strolling hand in hand among the beautiful flowers.
Somehow, I feel your presence here with me.
I know that is how God meant it to be.
Goodbye, my love, and when my work here
On earth is through,
God will take me home to be with you.

Burnell Burns L. Wood
Sumter, SC

My Expressions

Like the essence of a day gone by my expressions shattered, numb and saddened, like dark shadows of days gone by. My old world filled with gloom, misery, and despair.

Yet theirs the beautiful, untouched non-looked upon world of fulfillment, passion and legacies waiting to be found.

With castles so high that have a glow so bright that would make all dungeons of a mistful night glow.

As I walk along the deep mystic waters of crucial deeds and breaking hearts, I keep clinging to shreds of past expressions of love, joy, and laughter that can be equitted and heard from a silent dream.

A dream so vivid so real, like poison in a bottle waiting to be opened to be dropped upon me to fulfill my mind, to keep me sane only so I can keep on living in my dreams.

Malinda S. Lewis
Livingston, TN

Timeless poetry is. I am a mother of three handsome, wonderful boys, Alex, Zach, and Justin, and my dearest husband of twenty years, Ryan. I have written poetry all my life and did creative writing for my high school newspaper Highland High *in my home town of Anderson, IN. I am inspired by life and how out of all the good and bad, there is beauty, goodness, and love always right in front of us all the time. A special thanks to Eber & Wein Publishing, you have inspired me.*

Across the Way

November's Tale

Hush... hush...
The pine trees whisper,
For Old Man Winter's near,
He touched these woods,
Last night, you see
And brilliance disappeared.

Now gone,
The rubies, amber, gold,
Collected by the thief,
Who stole the jewels of autumn
To decorate his wreath.

The forest now
In muted cloak,
Wrapped up against the cold,
Will warn
Of winter's coming,
November's tale is told.

Heidi Kenney
Hubbarston, MA

First Day

I'm off today,
I'm on my way.
I will not cry,
I won't be shy.
Kindergarten will be a blast,
It's no problem I learn fast.
It's a time to play, read, and run,
There's no doubt I will have fun.
There will be books, projects to do,
A time for rest, a thought of you.
So, worry not when I'm not here,
I'll soon be home full of cheer.
I'll tell you all about my day,
Then you and I will sit and play!

Robin Dragoon
Plattsburgh, NY

Across the Way

Saving Myself

I dream of being an important person of today's society.
Giving back to the world that I know, as part of my recovery.
It all began growing up in the average middle class, loving home.
When I was just three, I began dancing up until the age of seventeen.
Throughout my years of dance, I became a black belt in the first degree.
Somehow, at the end of all of that I managed to take a turn down the wrong road.
My curiosity had been exposed, as my innocence unfolded.
I was now done pretending to be an angel, I was dying inside.
I was bullied middle school and named-called weirdo and bug eyes.
Becoming a teenager it all started to divide.
Running amuck, bad luck, rebellious, so what?
Intoxicating my intelligence, physical health and such.
I wasn't afraid, I was zoning out of touch.
I thought that I knew what I was doing.
All I was doing was not caring much.
Disengaging myself from negative associations, disconnecting all communications.
It was all fun and games first time around.
What a mess it left behind, people hurt and the consequences that surround.
There is another form of life outside of drugs and alcohol.
I'm loving life pure again, and I'm living more spiritual.
Today, I avoid burying my head in the sand, to avoid being put away in a can.
I had to change my way of life to see the future light.
I'm not missing out on life anymore.
I'm here now for my parents more than ever before.
I will preach until my days are done.
You're the only one who can save yourself, under this sun.

Melanie DiVincenzo
Haverhill, MA

I am an up-and-coming writer in poetry and as a lyricist. I am grateful for this opportunity to be heard, and to express my life experiences. Where I was, to where I am now, I'm not the only one, thousands can relate.

Brother's Beauty

In disarray for beauty searching deep,
Of time I spent, unmindful, all was waste.
From nothing came it; quick occurred its leap.
I realized beauty's meaning, then, in haste.

To grasp it seems the easy step in spite
Of complexity held in things so great.
Yet outer seen you cannot know its sight,
'Cause growth of beauty within stays innate.

In flowers, remained engulfed there I stayed,
Which, during, assumed beauty there was not;
In brother, shown a speck was—sadly nay!
In mine his eyes were, then my thoughts were fought.

My brother, beauty glows, it surrounds you.
Let's try to brightly start a better new.

Stacy Lamb
Natick, MA

Across the Way

Our Motivation

Do we want the truth
Or just to win
We will be our truth today
Will what we believe is the truth
Survive this day
Another given day
May reveal a different truth
But this is *the* day
The day chosen to count
We will be our truth today
On the same page
Make our mark
This is the day
There is no tomorrow
All moves have been calculated
All we need to do
Is execute
Please, sign the papers

Frankie Lee
Carnegie, PA

Fifty-eight, boilermaker, father (three), grandfather (nine), song writer, musician, and (she didn't) husband (1).

Long Flannel Gown

On a run-down farm 'bout a mile past town
An old couple lived, Sid and Elsie Brown
Their bodies were bowed by the sweat and tears
From tilling the soil nigh onto fifty years
The chill in the air and skies of gray
Told of a big snow heading their way
Sid, you can't go out in this weather today
I've got to Mama, a big snow is on the way
From daylight to dark he bedded taters down
The mist was freezing, time the sun went down
Supper was ready as he came in the door
Just coffee Mama, can't eat, my throat's sore
Mama, get out your long flannel gown
'Cause it looks like a hard winter coming down
Mama, lay close by me in your long flannel gown
With a chill and a fever seems, I'm coming down
Sid had never stirred come the break of day
Somehow Elsie knew he had passed away
As she stood close by while they put him in the ground
His words kept coming, but there was no sound
Mama lay close by me in your long flannel gown
'Cause it looks like a hard winter coming down

James E. Kelley
Gray, GA

I am a country boy poet who wrote my first poem in grade school. I was raised up during the Great Depression. My dad lost his farm and he moved to Georgia to work in the cotton mills. I wrote the "Long Flannel Gown" for Willie Nelson to use during his "Farm Aid Concerts." It tells of the end of a family farm with a twist and the hard life they led.

Across the Way

Eternity

Walking and gathering feelings
without aim in fate are fountains,
prospering in the frost whirlwinds
they which ascend on the dew
and take flight without remedy
to the mirrored waters' womb.

Existing in eternity, seeing
as fountains are reborn,
and in the endless elements
have been in cycles resting,
in the sun's virtue, all
flaming shadows are evaporating
embracing in recess, obedient
evolving crimsons on your cheeks.

Eternity exists in miniscule
journeys of October boughs,
leaving dreams when threading
in the infinite waters' depths
of new rebirths in due seasons.

Maria Pelaez
Tobyhanna, PA

Spilt

Eat your words since you're starving for attention
Wield them carefully, don't use them as a weapon
Words alone don't hurt, words alone can't heal
What matters in the end is how you make people feel

Spilling from your mouth
Spoiled down they rain
Hurtful their intent
What do you hope to gain
Acid to my ears
Toxic to my brain
You can mop them up, but the stain will still remain

Cut them with your sharp tongue
Choke on the shards of my broken heart
Truth lies in the pauses; little bits and parts
Said and then retracted
Forever they are spilt
Splattered across my psyche
Yours becomes my guilt

Denise S. Kinney
Gig Harbor, WA

Across the Way

Family

These walls are a secure gate
We have not been here since last state
It is the blood that forever flows
Within the river no one knows

Ride above highs and under lows
Silence is where the wind blows
How fortunate it is to be someone
Who stands firm beneath the burning sun

Who cares if I eat too much
It is the blood within my touch
My mind is still, yet running fast
Made to be a lone outcast

Lay me down to go to sleep
The wormhole's becoming much too deep
At least I have not drawn a dud
Had I, I would have extracted blood

Instead I will concentrate
On winning this long debate
About how one should listen to hear
Whenever the thickest of blood is near

Connect all the dots together
Then polish it to shiny leather
Need to stay strong through each birth
So our blood can remain on Earth.

Gregory M. Musto
Schenectady, NY

The Sea Cave

A cave lies stone deep
where a warm song plays,
on the walls it creeps,
on waters it lays.

The sound and domain are joined—
a deep sonorous wave of soprano
trumpeting on torrid dome—
undulating rhythm, soothing echo.

Massive, rough monuments of rock
sheathed in glimmering sea,
protruding, rigid face to stalk,
stone, music, amity.

Notes and waves sweeping salty skin,
last abode of wandering foam and sea,
I, trudging above Ocean's bin
to the sea god's palace, dulcet and free.

Amanda E. Hartsell
Orlando, FL

Across the Way

Darling

Darling, shut your eyes and sway.
Don't care about what they think,
because it's okay to be gay.

Don't let them ruin your day.
Their judgements add only a kink.
Darling, just shut your eyes and sway.

I promise you those bullies will pay.
Stop feeling like you want to shrink,
because it's okay to be gay.

I promise you I will slay
all those bullies who put you on the brink.
Darling, just shut your eyes and sway.

Don't be so gray.
Look in that mirror and wink,
because it's okay to be gay.

It's going to be okay.
Here's a glass, take a drink.
Darling, just shut your eyes and sway,
because it's okay to be gay.

Franquie Hallczuk
Biddeford, ME

God Made You My Mother

God made you my mother
To raise and take care of me

God made you my mother
To love and stand by me

God made you my mother
Because He knew you are the best

God made you my mother
So I could have someone to turn to

God made you my mother
Because I would love you the best

God made you my mother
Because He knew we would be close

God made you my mother
Because you are the perfect one

Theresa Chadwick
Toledo, OH

Across the Way

One Voice

Freaks seen in silent voice
Twisted are the words that anchor rhythm and rhyme
Unjust to magnification for all to see
I have no voice I am mute

Once driven now dead
How dare you question?!
How dare you voice?!
How dare you?!

Placed like figures on cake
The all stands ready
Dissecting each piece useless
Over the cliff they go

A faint sound buried, buried, buried
Voice it Voice no more
Searching to hear what wasn't said
I finally speak it out loud!

Marcella Gae Robertson
Medford, OR

I am a fifty-three-year-old woman, retired police lieutenant. I have a beautiful son, Darryl, daughter-in-law, Ericka, and grandbabies, Corryn and Colton. I am blessed to have strong and supportive family and friends. Honestly, I did not write this poem alone—meaning it felt as if something of higher consciousness came right through me in about three minutes, and I only made spelling corrections. I have come to realize there is nothing more important than how we treat each other and ourselves. To understand, that past all the layers, we are all "love" no matter what! Period!

will you hear me?

will you hear me if i cry
above the thunder of anger
over blast of fear and hate
when help doesn't come
or when it comes too late?
when streets explode with anger
and love becomes hate
and hearts grow dead
when all the sounds are down?
will you hear me if i cry?
will you come before i die?

James A. Potts
Memphis, TN

Found

I stood like a tree on the wind-blown land above the sea.
The crashing waves on the rocks sent spray onto me.
The rain washed my soul, thunder and lightning crashed about me.
Yet I was strengthened by my roots firmly embedded in the land,
and I was made happy and wise allowing me to see all the beauty
around me, living or not.
Then I knew I was free, not to be controlled by any I allowed not
to control. Though I was an orphan, I found my parents to be the
world.

David R. Mason
Heneford, AZ

Across the Way

Only Worse Remains

For better or for worse
Nervously cast towards a wide open sun
Left adrift to sink to the sea floor of the soul
Forgotten to erode among the salt of time
Until a dark ship's light shines

Raised into the cold ocean wind
Only worse remains
Carved into a weathered map of pain
Better dissolves in the swirling sands
Victim to the current of a moon's unconscious plan

Alan Horsnail
Denver, CO

Alan is an award-winning screenwriter and poet. He currently lives in Denver, CO.

Digital Dreams

Fidgeting with digital dreams
Not everything is what it seems
Beautiful bushes and luscious lawns
Vibrant views and pretentious palms
They're all just numbers and beams
Don't be fooled by how it seems
The beautiful bushes are just a program
Luscious lawns are simply a graphic
The vibrant views are only an Instagram
Pretentious palms have a little static
You may find a person you like,
I'm trying to warn you, so you won't put up a fight
You'll think your love is true
Because it'll all feel brand new
But the only true love that could ever be true
Is the one that involves me and you
Please don't get sucked into digital dreams
Believe me, it's not what it seems.
You may think that perfection surrounds you, but not quite.
Come back to where the bushes are luscious
and the lawns are beautiful,
not a pixel in sight.
Please come back, I need you
And you, you need me too.
This digital dream is nothing, soon you'll see
Nothing is real, not even me

Tristan Liam Durham
Spring, TX

Across the Way

A Rose by Any Other Name

A Rose by any other name should sound as sweet,
As sweet as the red lollipops she reminds me of,
As sweet as the glassy cherries hanging from the trees,
Just as sweet...
A Rose by any other name should be as pure,
As pure as the very water that grew her.
A Rose by any other name should be as soft
Soft as the hair on a newborn's crown,
But I know of no Rose by this name.
I know of a Rose who shot up quickly
Her sharp prickly thorns ripping through the soil.
I know of a Rose that broke the ground when she came,
Who sprouted even when there was no rain,
Who moves even when there is no wind.
I know of a Rose whose petals were not red
But stained with purple,
Symbolizing the death that everyone thought would become of her.
A Rose by any other name should sound as sweet
But me?
I know of no such Rose.

Amanda R. Ravello
Queens, NY

A Love for All

I have a love for all artists
Musicians, sketch artists, visual artists
Painters, sculptors
Etc., etc.
Art is my first love
But artists are my second attraction
I can't promise you will fall in love with every song
each melody but I will make sure that every time
that pencil touches the paper
that it sketches out the words "You Have My Heart"
I want your eyes to visualize that I'm all about You and I
I can't promise my paint brush will paint the prettiest picture
but It will try to capture the essence of how I feel just right
My hands will sculpt this image of a love so true a sunset so serene
and a sunrise you only wish you could see daily
Art is my poetry she is my first love
but her artistic phrase is my second attraction
and on this February 14th day people call Valentine's Day
I want you to know your whole being is beautiful
and whether you want to strum each guitar string
or paint canvases all day know
That my feelings for you still remain the same
because I love the artist in you and that won't change

Dominique Michelle Washington
Newark, CA

Across the Way

As Souls Live On

Those who died were those who lived
Who lost their lives with lots to give
And those who live refuse to die
While those alive accept a lie
With death be close and death be near
Your end at most which ends in tears
When those who loved and those who lost
With bodies cleansed and souls that crossed
Can't cheat death can't be escaped
With peace at rest and life will wait
Inside the grave inside the tomb
The souls who crave cause lots of doom
And those who died remain a life
That's left behind and left to die
A further death that's worse than all
A death at best who took the fall
One last breath and one last fall
The cause of death, result of all
For it seeks all when all is numb
When Satan calls, your time has come
Suffer more or suffer less
After death, eternal rest
Buried deep into the ground
Silent screams and faded sounds

Joshua M. Barnett
Bakersfield, CA

My name is Joshua Michael Barnett. I have always loved art and decided that I wanted to do art in my future. My talents are that I can draw, paint, sculpt, rap, dance, I do a little literature. I've been put down a lot but didn't let that get to me; I keep trying. I'd like to thank my family for believing me and some of my friends who actually think I have a future. I've been abused by my ex-stepdads, physically and mentally, and got my brother, Billy Massey taken by CPS.

Cold Actuality

It's like you're fading from my mind.
Ugh, my mind.
What is it with my mind?
It's like everything is lost and I have nothing to find.
My heart grows heavy, it feels like stone.
They say, "You're grown."
I'm supposed to be grown;
yet I feel so small.

Is that all?
They tell me, "You can't fight,
Don't fight, lower your fists,
you can't fight the fall."
They left me without real words,
Lies slapped in my face,
Then tell me to embrace.
Embrace?

You rule me like a prisoner, yet I could almost be queen.
There has to be truth, something in between?
Fading from my consciousness,
Melting from reality,
Forgiveness in cold actuality.
Once the beat of my heart, the spark of my soul,
Putting the pistol to my mind,
No longer whole.

Jacquelyne G. Carrillo
Phoenix, AZ

Across the Way

Easter Egg

The Easter lilies showed so happy
Above the glorious pathways of roses.
They glistened with the love of many,
And glowed with the hope from us all.

A hidden egg,
Coloured blue and pink,
Sat quietly behind the stems so tall.

The children, dressed in clothes so pretty,
Ran around the grass so green.
The boys and girls all joyous and happy,
Searching for those eggs hidden
By the Easter Bunny.

The hidden egg,
Resting there, waiting,
Just waiting.
The children came closer,
And closer to her.

A little girl, in a bright blue dress,
Exclaimed, so cheerfully,
"I found the best Easter egg ever!"

Easter D. Morgan
St. Louis, MO

Life Goes On

Young hands
Do not yet understand
Innocent and scared
Cannot yet bare
The world that isn't fair
First love
First time being crushed
Swearing to never love again
Hoping that their broken heart will mend
Life goes on
They now understand what it is to be strong
Aged hands
Holding their love
Teary eyes
When their love dies
Sitting alone
Broken and old
Waiting for their last breath
To kiss the earth goodbye
And join their love
In the sky

Hannah K. Pratt
Oakford, IL

Across the Way

Trees of Winter

Ode to the strength
of the trees of winter.
Ode to the satisfying decay
of gray matted branches.
Ode to the worshipful flow
of the branches upward.
Ode to the diversity
of its roadside constituents.
Ode to deciduous brother
and evergreen sister.
Ode to those laid bare
and those covered still.
Ode to the dying canopy
and the virgin earth floor.
Ode to the stark exposure
of barren limbs.
Ode to the sweet lichen
and needy parasite friends.
Ode to the transparent ugliness
and the breathtaking splendor.
Ode to the strength
of the trees of winter.

Kari Wilhite
Bonney Lake, WA

Idiot Savant

Idiot savant though I be
Writing the words that I see
Pulling them out of thin air
A wizard of words if you dare

All emotions set on high
Taking control from the inside
Led with a burning desire
Feeling in my soul, bringing the fire

But the words are just a trail
The path chosen guides my sail
Taking me to uncharted thoughts
World class thief who is never caught

My world of words makes me king
With all the power that it brings
A perfect world in my mind
like my spirit, one of a kind

Anthony David Johnson
Fair Oaks, CA

Across the Way

Something About a Sunrise

There is something about a sunrise
That speaks of a new glory day,
Something about each tendril of light
And every vivid sun-ray.

There is something about the colors
That speak of an Artist's brush,
Something in each careful hue
To make Lady Dawn blush.

There is Someone in the heavens
Who takes care to paint the morn,
Someone who loves all —
Be they happy, sad, or worn.

There is Someone in the heavens,
Ever near, unseen by earthly eyes,
Whose Light shines through days' end
And wakes again come sunrise.

Sarah E. Dake
Niota, TN

The Wall

This wall of stone, I built to protect me when I'm all alone
Nobody is going to tear me down
See that's where you messed up baby
Because what goes around comes back around
Trying to read me, tripping about what you see
But you can't believe there's a wall in front of me

There's no time for regret, well better yet, I'll keep pushing
    through
Not revealing the healing I'm dwelling
Back up man! I refuse to be hurt again
Swallowed the key to my heart when I wanted to depart
To take time to find myself, my spiritual being, and life's meaning

This wall built out of stones
Surrounding this heart-shaped muscle between my bones
Consistently pounding
Craving for the wind that blows, resisting the feeling within
Damn wall won't let anyone in
Love blocked, trust blocked, caring locked in

All these cuts people have caused
Healing, these Band-Aids I'm pealing
But never again
When this wall keeps that pain from beginning once again…

Destiny C. Hicks
Frisco, TX

Across the Way

My Lighthouse

My lighthouse even knows there's more than what is told.
Sharks keep swimming,
I'm no longer in fear,
I've swum to the shore,
Where none of you seem to exist here.
Safe inside, I climbed my lighthouse,
As I approached the lookout, I glanced down south.
Peering into the ocean,
As if it's a torturous place I never have been.
I stood upon the edge of my lighthouse,
Waving down south,
Farewell my sins, I am free at last.
My lovely lighthouse has rescued me,
No more hiding,
I'll shine with its lighting.
Lighting up the night,
Standing tall and striking all the demons of the sea.
Balancing high above,
As I am free.
My lighthouse knows me and holds me close,
My armory that I love the most.
Built up in bricks,
The walls are thick.
Incapable of being knocked down, my beautiful lighthouse stood tall,
Waiting patiently as the recovery of my fall.

Courtney Casteel
Hillsboro, MO

Once Upon a Time

Hair the color of the midnight sky,
Glancing off the feathers of a raven's wing.
His skin glistening with the promise of a new day,
Along with each whispered oath he would say.
Fairy tales once came true,
Once upon a time,
But not even Prince Charming could save me now,
As I fell mesmerized by his pools of endless blue. I never
believed I'd fall in love,
Given thanks to painful tragedies,
Removing from my life the ones I loved,
My world,
My light, my peace.
But when his touch echoed the thoughts of my own,
Mirroring the things I wish I had shown,
Once upon a time,
An unspoken truce displayed for all,
Our love that always shone.
When I wasn't fighting for my life,
I wallowed away in broken silence,
Surrounded by my flowing tears,
Shed for the one I came to love,
Who had me strung so tight.
The one I couldn't help but free,
For there were many others greater than me.

Kaitlyn Hooley
Lodi, CA

My name is Kaitlyn Hooley and I'm eighteen years old. I started writing my first book when I was the early age of twelve. I self-published that short novel at thirteen. I started really writing poetry on a daily basis when I experienced my first heartbreak. Poetry helps me describe what I'm going through. It helps me through challenges in getting my emotions together. I enjoy playing piano, writing poetry, novels, and music, drawing, reading, and singing. I was home schooled and graduated at the age of sixteen through my own personal study and determination.

Across the Way

Loss

"Grammy died"
I sat quietly
Heard Mom cry
Couldn't think
Had to comfort Mom

I walked back into my room half an hour later
Sat on my own bed
Still in a state of shock
Couldn't think. Couldn't breathe
My heart was a tsunami of emotions
A new streak of pain with each wave

How could someone with such a loving heart die?
I screamed and sobbed
Eventually came to my senses
Had to go to school
Depressed all day
No one noticed

Why are the people with the strongest, everlasting love gone first?
When all the hateful people are left alone
To cause all the kind hearts pain
To twist the knife ever so slowly
As to cause the most pain

Samaya O. Rubio
Redondo Beach, CA

The Vaughan Song

There comes a time in everyone's life
When they must call it an end
It's a shame the best are taken first
And the rest get to do it again
I remember the time in Alpine Valley
We came to hear them play
There was Robert and Erick
And Stevie Ray Vaughan
That went on that day
Stevie was at the end of his tour
And was going home for a stay
When the chopper he was on had some trouble
And went down that day
Well I met him just a month before
In St. Paul Minnesota
He smiled at me and shook my hand
Before he had to go
What was the cause of the crash that day?
Does anyone really know?
Your soul will live forever
You've given so much of it

Rick Rhythm Williams
Brooklyn Center, MN

I'm a singer, song writer, musician and poet. I have published and recorded my work and received several awards. I have been published in twenty international poetry books, received six Editor's Choice awards, one Accomplishment of Merit award, an International Poet of Merit award, the 2012 International Who's Who in Poetry award, and 2012 Best Poets and Poems award. I have been on the radio and have played music on stage with several well-known blues musicians. One of the biggest crowds I have played in front of was over five thousand people. My home is in Minneapolis, MN, but most of all my family is my first passion and number one love.

Across the Way

Death in Life

It's that anything
 You'd give
 For something
 To feel

Pure silence in an empty room
Broken breathing in a crowded skull
 In the death of a thought
  Another is brought to life
   Another is brought to life

Conversation in a crowded room
Broken breathing in a crowded skull
 In a moment of weakness
  Another is brought to life
   Pride is sentenced to death

It's that anything
 You'd give
  To feel
Nothing

   Reincarnated
To be sentenced to death
    Reincarnated
Incapable of comprehending
 The relentlessness of perfection.

Madison E. Kraus
Farmington Hills, MI

The Tainted Snow

The lamb plays night and day.
She's soft, she's sweet, and she's ever gay.
She's with her mother, but yearns to go astray.
For danger lurks not far away —

The lion perched up on a rock.
He's keeping an eye on this forbidden flock.
At this pristine lamb he gawks —
This lamb he begins to sweet talk.

The little lamb goes with this lion.
For his eyes lure her as though they're made of diamond.
He and she climb up the highland.
So quiet, so clean, as though they escaped to an island.

The little lamb starts to cry.
For his touch is not right —
But no one shall hear, for they're too out of sight.
The little lamb tries to make flight.

The lion is proud of his difficult find.
With one hit, the little lamb's blind.
He enjoys this powerful state of mind.
For on her he dined.

Canaan M. Voss
New Haven, MO

I saw a match; I lit it. I hope I can start a fire that will, one day, cover the whole world. Help spread my fire.

Across the Way

Change

Change can be big
Or change can be small
Like the transition of summer to fall
Fall to winter
Winter to spring
The seasons always change
But that's only one thing

Change for the better
Change for the worse
That great new dress
Or hideous new purse

Change can be life
Or change can be death
The baby's beginning
The old man's last breath

Change is there
Whether in seconds or minutes
Just open your eyes
And try not to miss it
Once there's change
There's no going back
You keep moving forward
Like a train on a track

Elizabeth A. MacEnulty
Saint Louis, MO

Last Breath

The world is black.
The words are white.
Life is no match for the
parasite of dead bite.
Take one last breath
as you're about to face death
in front of hell's gates and then
there's Heaven's door.
Swimming to the shore, the shore
of all regret lay before.
I've paid my dues. I've paid my price.
I feel as if I've died twice.
When the angels swoop down,
I lay with no sound.
Motionless.
Motionless I lay.
And there I stay until the end of time.

Micayla Snyder
Walnutport, PA

My name is Micayla, and I am fifteen years old. I write poetry to help express myself, and to get my emotions out on paper. The rest of my poetry is inspired by my love of music. I hope you enjoyed my poem as much as I loved writing it.

Across the Way

Within Herself

She smiles she knows she feels it coming.
It knocks tells her let me in.
She screams no one hears her, she's all alone.
It comes closer, cherishes her face, she closes her eyes,
she's been here before. She thought she escaped it,
she thought she ran,
so much comes, so little can see.
She closes her eyes as her blood is flooding,
she feels it but doesn't dare to scream again.
She feels the hunger, the anger that it feels,
she has tried to be good to live for God.
But everyone said she was a failure.
She smiles; she knows what power she will have.
Inside her, she soon won't feel all the confusion;
it was always there deep within her.
She loves but they don't care,
she tells but they don't hear.
So this time she is escaping, she is letting it in.
As all her blood is drained from her soul,
she can't feel, she is numb. Then she smiles, rips it up,
says if you can't believe in me,
if you want to break me down.
Now, now it is my time to set free,
I am coming, coming for you.
Don't you fear what I have become;
soon, soon your pain will be over.
You won't feel it, my dear child,
soon you will be with me,
and she closes her eyes, and whispers, "Within myself."

Mirela Hadziomerovic
Des Moines, IA

I was born in a war and after that my family had struggles coming to America. Once we came here, my family only had five dollars in their pocket and they left their whole family behind for a better future for my sister and me. With them being so brave and strong, this is what has inspired me to write my poems.

He

He lays his head against the concrete
And lets coolness seep into his skin
Behind him is the roar of the city's street
But his mind is somewhere else within

He beats himself up with self hatred
No one can understand
This hole that his depression created
To him, he's already damned

He writes atrocious stories of rage
That reflect his affliction
You could never comprehend a single page
Thinking that it was fiction

He is isolated and unknown
Just the way he likes
Someone you always condone
Lest he makes a single strike

He shows his pain in mysterious ways
For you could never see
The mind he obtains is a drunken haze
And is littered with torturous debris

If you don't understand who I am talking about
My friend, a secret I will let you in
But the story I have told you, do not flout
For "he" is really you deep within

Beza Townsend
Kokomo, IN

Across the Way

Snowflake

A snowflake, what a beautiful sight.
A shimmering diamond on a cold winter's night.
On its own, a magical bright.
Altogether, lost in plain sight.
A snowflake is who they are,
Gracefully landing on a hood of a car.
So let's act like a snowflake and be ourselves.
Snowflakes are lost, but memories are held.

Benjamin Joseph Miller
Middleton, WI

Fingernails

Step right up and choose your fingernails.
Nails, nails, nails.
Pretty nails, glamorous nails.
Painted nails, pictured nails.
Flowers, doves, rainbows.
Glitter nails!
Glitzy nails!
Red, white and blue nails.
Square, round and black nails.
Long, short and white nails.
Hard as nails?
Go ahead. Step right up.
Choose your special fingernails.

Linda Furniss-Jones
Pendleton, OR

To a Spring Warbler

After winter's long and painful cold, you appeared.
Your music brought spring's bright, joyous warmth.
It filled my soul with its passion
And healed my wounded heart with its love.

Rose M. Rogers
Rico, CO

The warbler appeared in early spring as winter was releasing its hold. A Southerner, I had spent the past months in New Jersey with my sister as she struggled with a terminal illness. She loved the feathered friends who nested, fed, and sang outside her kitchen window. She knew each bird and could whistle each individual song. The songs, including hers, had been silent throughout the winter. The poem expressed the joy of the warbler's visit. A retired teacher, I have lived in Texas and in Nashville, TN. At present, I reside in the San Juan Mountains in Colorado.

Across the Way

Under Your Silhouette

There's a story in your silhouette
I wish so badly to uncover
So put on that fine, defining jacket of yours
And let's get to know each other
With our feet falling in step
We tour the changing leaves of fall trees
Then sit down for a mug of tea
Slowly your lines become more defined
But how about you take off that fine, defining jacket of yours
And let's get to know each other
I wish so badly to read the story under your silhouette
Please let me in
Where the secrets cling to the skeleton
Under your skin
Please let me in

Maddi Mueller
Seattle, WA

Mockingbird

The mockingbirds had stopped singing.
The leaves fell silently on the morning dew.
The sun had stopped shining.
The stars weren't as bright as they once were.
I watched you leave
as the stars faded
and the sunlight no longer came through the curtains.
By now,
you could be happy.
I hope you are.
The mockingbirds still sing for you.
The leaves fall delicately on the morning dew grass.
The sun has shined brighter
and the stars are bright each night just for you.
You could be happy,
and I suppose you are.

Daphnie I. Rodriguez
San Antonio, TX

Across the Way

Phoenix

He watched her as she watched him
He of fire and she of skin
He spread his wings as she raised her arms
He of flames and she of charm
He bowed his head as she bowed hers too
He of old ashes and she of earth once new
He sprang high as she crouched low
He of billowing light and she of skin like snow
He sang without words as she sang with them
He of crackling echoes and she of musical hymn
He perched near her as she began to sway
He of whispered folk tales and she of the very day
He came close as she leaned to touch
He of blazing heat and she who felt no such
And then they wondered what they were
A great bird aflame
And a girl unnerved
And then she fell—
Fell into him
Became the Phoenix
And he, the Human

Brandi N. Anderson
Flagstaff, AZ

Angels' Wings

When you came to this world not long ago
Angels brought you, so we were told
On angels' wings your life began
Placed gently in your mother's hands

The angels watched over you day and night
And on their wings your dreams took flight
Above the clouds and so far to go
On angels' wings of silver and gold

Your life has come and gone too soon
Leaving us with just and empty room
Filled with memories of you
And a heavenly light above the gloom

Angels' wings are now your own
Angels' wings of silver and gold
Flying high and free up to Heaven
You go to where your life was given

Georgette M. Clark
Azle, TX

I wrote this poem for everyone who has died before their life was complete.

Across the Way

Keep Your Faith

You go through trials and tribulations just to test your faith
Hold on tight, things will be all right, His love will pull you
 through
With Jesus in your life there's nothing you can't do
His hand is on you day by day to help lead you through
All I have is yours and I thank you Lord
With all the blessings you give, we take them all in praise
Through right and wrong you hold our hand to keep us from going
 astray
Read the only book and do as it's been written
When people say to show me give your heart to thee
When people say to prove me, He will make you free
He'll help you with your problems, He'll give comfort, all you need
No left, no right, just walk straight to show your faith to He
He died for all our sins, with praise we should show Him
So just watch and see, our faith is all we need

That's all we'll ever need

Dan Cravener
Hyde Park, PA

The Flood

In the sky
A raindrop on the windowpane
   I am harmful just the same
I and a billion more
   On a trip to the ocean shore
Gravity is our master
   So we must go faster
We pick up a tin can and carry it along
   We are getting strong
Now we are a raging river
   Our power makes men quiver
Our size grows many times more
   Hell bent for the ocean shore
We are a natural force
   All is destroyed without remorse
Homes, bridges, cars and all
   If man made it, it will fall
Our crest will come — it will recede
   All may see the grizzly deed
Man will return and look
   But never learn
Nature needs space as well as him
   Remember Nature never gives in
Remember I was a raindrop on a windowpane.

John R. Bramley
Delhi, NY

Across the Way

My Grandma

My grandma, she's so good to me, I know she loves me so.
She tells the greatest stories about the long ago.

She bakes the greatest cookies a fellow ever ate,
And always has enough for me to share with each playmate.

She always knows the nicest things to do upon a rainy day,
To entertain a fellow and pass the time away.

And as I grow older, she seems to understand
I must make mistakes and stumble, but she calmly holds my hand.

And if I had just one wish, I would wish one very line,
I would wish that everyone could find a grandma just like mine.

Velda Mason-Davis
Bronston, KY

The Silent Cat

The silent cat sat at the window
And never meowed
The quiet dog sat by the door
And never barked

The old man and woman sat on the porch
And never talked
The children play on the lawn
And never made any noise

The cars went by
But never blew their horns

The quiet dog
The old man and woman who never talked
The children who never made any noise
The cars that never blew their horn

While the little deaf girl looked on

Allielou Patricia Ann Campbell
Hartland, NB Canada

Poetry writing has provided countless hours of enjoyment for me. Poetry is my way of expressing my appreciation of the beauty around us; my feelings and innermost thoughts. I also express my feelings through other writing, painting and photography. I have a big collection of my writings and artwork. It has been very rewarding. Again, thank you for this opportunity to have my work published in your book.

Across the Way

Lost Love

I can't tell you I love you, I can't say I do.
Losing you will be the hardest thing I've ever had to do.
Crying, sighing, dying on the inside,
it's so hard to say goodbye.
The snow is coming down.
I wish we were together,
but you left and the snow is still here,
and I will be broken forever.
I can't say I love you, I can't say I do.
Losing you is the hardest thing I've had to do.
When will it be spring so I can start over?

Hateful, harsh, hollow words are said how do I fix this?
You say goodbye, I can't unravel this in my head.
I sit in my bed thinking that you and I were going to wed.
I can't tell you I love you, I can't say I do
because you are gone and I have to move on from you.
Your door is closed and another one will open.
when you come back, I will be gone.
I won't tell you I love you, that won't do.

Emily Rose Nagyvathy
Northville, MI

Imagine

Imagine Jesus as he hung on the tree,
not a sin or a fault had He.
A crown of thorns upon His head,
no doubt the blood ran down His face,
was anger there?! No, not a trace.
He could have called 10,000 angels,
but He hung there and died for strangers.
He knew what He had to do that day
He knew man's fate was at stake.
They spit on Him and called Him names
those evil men knew no shame.
His garment they parted at His feet
as He looked on lowly and meek.
They pierced him deep within His side,
Father forgive, He cried,
Then He hung His head and died.
Imagine.

Alice F. McGraw
Waldo, AR

Across the Way

Lost

I sit and wait to be enfolded
I lie still and hold my heart
I don't reach, don't touch, don't hold another
Only in my dreams.
I don't hope, don't look, don't long for
Only when unseen.
Yes, I sit and wait and wonder
Believing illusions, rejecting truth
And soon the rhythm
Echoes, fades, dies.

Terri-Karlene P. Peart
Florence, SC

Ralph's Conquest

There once was a penguin
named Ralph
who always sat on the shelf
(since he had
no feathers from his mother!)

But then one day, a new
"coat" was made—for him—
and now he can swim
with the others!

Carol Whelan
Glendale, AZ

It's Up to You

In one moment everything has become so different
Close friends are now so distant
And the ones I never thought I could find are by my side
I believe it is a sign.
God smiled and gave me something one of a kind
I know this because he gave me you
He tested us by giving us everything we have gone through
Nothing has changed and that should prove something
But we haven't finished, until the test of someone else comes
You have fallen in love and it kills me to know this
I see what is going on and you feel complete bliss
I want to tell you it is a lie, but how can I do that
Any chance of me ever having those feelings fell flat
But when I see you I wish it weren't true
We are losing something that people spend a lifetime trying to find
A perfect friendship...soon to be gone
I know you don't know what to do now because you can't have us both
This is when the true question will come
Do you keep your best friend or a girl who you think is the one
There are sayings that go along with this issue
But I won't say them, in case I would offend you
I know who I would choose and this has nothing to do with me
But as long as you're happy
That is all I want for you
I have told you this before and I hope you know this
I don't want you to forget me, but I'd rather you have bliss
I hope you don't forget your best friend because of one girl's kiss.

Emily Botta
Fort Lauderdale, FL

Across the Way

Your Smiling Face

Your smiling face
is my sunshine
It rained the
other day
Your warmth and beauty
brightened through
and chased the clouds
away
Your glowing eyes
Your tenderness
Your charm and
kindness too
All help me to
realize
Why I'm so fond
of you
And should some
clouds appear again
and darken my
sunlight skies
I'll think of you
and you alone and watch the
clouds drift by

John Van Ness
Stony Point, NY

My name is John Van Ness. I am sixty-five years of age. I am a high school graduate and I attended two years of college at Rockland Community College in Rockland County, Suffern, New York. I was in an English 101 course, an English composition course and my instructor was also a poet who encouraged us to write. His name is Daniel Masterson and is currently the Poet Laureate of Rockland County. The poem that I wrote was a result of a quarrel that I had with my girlfriend.

Two Is Better Than One

Two is better than one, as the saying goes,
and having twin sons, only Matt and Kelly know.
They may have been born on the very same day,
But traits and personalities differ in every way.
Remember your lives came together, two people fell in love,
Because of total commitment, you've been
blessed from God above.

Gloria E. Schmitt
Racine, WI

I am a sixty-eight-year-young woman who enjoys writing poetry, especially for a special occasion. My husband and I will celebrate our seventh wedding anniversary in September. He is a World War II Veteran. His granddaughter and her husband were blessed with twin boys. Instead of a store-bought card to give with the gift, I wrote this poem.

Across the Way

Can We All Just Get Along Now?

No matter what race, creed,
or color in God's sight we are all
sisters and brothers.
We are all here for a common purpose:
love and understanding.
If I have harmed you in any manner,
whatever it is, tell me,
talk to me.
No one else knows my journey
through life but God   and me.
He put us here for a common purpose.
It doesn't matter
what language you speak or
country you are from,
all that matters
at the end of the day is love...
for each other.

Lola Maire Boutte
Houston, TX

Retrospectively

When we look back at our life
We wonder how we did in strife,
Take the ups and downs,
The minuses and the pluses.
We wonder what happened to our dreams,
How we tackled all the realms,
The highs, the lows,
Successes and negative blows.

We walked through life rather happily
Seeing it as vermilion,
Often paying no mind
Like Ornithopods sixty-five million years ago,
When their future was still secure.
Hope was our guide
And mostly we were right.
In retrospect, the bad is half forgotten,
The good stays with us,
We are still besotten.

J. Emmi Janotha
North Huchinson Island, FL

Across the Way

A Reflection of Life

I look back on life and see it as a flicker in time,
As a firefly that glows for only a brief time.
The thrill of wonder in a child's eyes at Christmas.
Remembering the excitement of getting your first bicycle,
and the accomplishment of riding it all the way down the block.
The anticipation of receiving a report card with your first
"A" grade, and feeling a sense of jubilation.
The first time for "puppy love," when butterflies are all a
flutter in one's tummy, over the feelings of another person.
Oh, the innocence of time, where did it go?

Big city lights captivate the young and eager at heart.
Like the achievement one feels of accepting their first job.
Then, learning the lesson about the money tree. "What comes in,
must go out."

How happy is the day when the love of your life appears.
You embrace every moment together. Like a colorful sunset in
shades of pink, orange and yellow hues. The sense of tranquility
and peace calms the soul. Then as autumn turns to winter, the
heart stokes a lifetime of memories.

Looking back on the reflection of life gives pause, to realize
with a grateful heart, just how precious life can be.

Kelly Rogers
Santee, CA

I create poetry from the depths of my heart, which is where an abundance of life experiences are.

Still the Best

Twenty-eight years we never fought,
a cross word there was not.
Twenty-eight years our friendship did endure,
for every problem this was the cure.
I miss your funny stories,
and all your gracious glories.
The way you made the wacky faces,
With you always the happiest of places.
People always all around,
a home just full of sound.
Kids all over just runnin',
adults outside just sunnin'.
I think about it day and night,
how you left us just not right,
the end of this life was not in sight.
When I visit you there in the ground,
I close my eyes and hear your voice,
it's all around.
And then as if by choice,
you rustle leaves or branches making sound.
You tell me to look in the sky,
Now you've sprouted wings and fly!
The words we always share,
I'll be all right as long as I know you're there.
My heart sings, you're here!

Rose Rodgers
Titusville, PA

Dedicated to Cathy, everyone's best friend, but I hold the privilege of being called her best friend.

Across the Way

When There Is Love

When there is love
there is no holding grudges

When there is love
there is always caring

When there is love
there is always a time to share

When there is love
there is always a smile to give

When there is love
there is always someone to talk to

When there is love
there is always a shoulder to cry on

When there is love
there is always a family to turn to

When there is love
there is always forgiveness

When there is love
there is always you

Mary Laurina
Woodbridge, NJ

Go for a Run with Your Daughter

Go for a run with your daughter
Or a walk.
Stride in silence for a time
And truly be with her.

The mountains glisten in the distance
And echo their approval
As we bridge the path.

Together.
One leading the other
And then, reversing fortunes,
Following the other's swath.

The breathing quickens.
Almost a gasp,
and we share moments
in which transformation
takes us away from the pack.

What gets transformed,
the skeptic plaintively cries?
And we embrace our rhythm.
Look to the sky.
And quietly own
the victories in our lives.

Fred Bapp
Centennial, CO

Index of Poets

A

Abernathy, Nancy E. 61
Abramczyk, Augusta 70
Agee-Herring, Lois 190
Alexander, Gail A. 59
Alto, Elina 4
Anderson, Brandi N. 304
Anderson, Elizabeth 241
Anderson, Fern R. 47
Andrasko, Nicole 250
Anselmo, Robert L. 15
Anselona, Phyllis M. 2
Anteau, Janice M. 239
Armbrust, James D. 11
Armellino, Rachel 131
Atristain, Javier 85

B

Bailey, Sara 247
Bapp, Fred 321
Barnett, Joshua M. 282
Bearss, Carol A. 182
Beck, Julie 84
Beckrow, Hailey 97
Bedner, Michael S. 259
Berry, Deonette 72
Bessler, William P. 20
Bevins, Whitney B. 57
Birmingham, Sharon A. 46
Blagburn, Dajani 212
Boring, Martha M. 71
Botta, Emily 313
Boulware, Winthrop O. 123
Boutte, Lola Maire 316
Boyd, Vera R. 118
Bramley, John R. 307
Braswell, Kathy 205
Briseno, Alicia D. 174
Brown, Carolyn 254
Brown, Ted 77
Brown, William C. 200
Bryla, Helen L. 42
Burkhalter, Charles F. 80
Burkhart, Carol 55

C

Caldwell, Vernessa 232
Cameron, Jeffrey 40
Campbell, Allielou Patricia Ann 309
Candelaria, Gloria 238
Canevari, Leonore 7
Carbo, Lois 6
Carey, Lou A. 146
Carlovich, Ann 143
Carr, Guyola 41
Carr, Marsha 155
Carrillo, Jacquelyne G. 283
Carter, Brianna 100
Casteel, Courtney 290
Chadwick, Theresa 275
Chromey, Paul A. 152
Clark, Georgette M. 305
Clifford, Tina J. 39
Coates, Gary L. 216
Cole, Kathy 117
Coleman, Darian 16
Collins, Barbara J. 33
Copeland, Lisa 136
Corbett, Clare Ellen 54
Cort, Lew 22
Craig, Benjamin Z. 240
Cravener, Dan 306
Crawford, LeAnn 176
Cresto, Karen 214
Cross, Artie R. 90

D

D'Aiutolo, Mary 215
Dake, Sarah E. 288
Davis, Roy V. 231
DeHaven, Susie 24
Delaney, Peter 52
Devulapalli, Krishna 245
DiVincenzo, Melanie 266
Dixon, Julia M. 38
Dooley, Evelyn 147
Dragoon, Robin 265
DuBose, Judith 23
Duff, Leah A. 56
Durham, Janie M. 101
Durham, Tristan Liam 279
Dyer, David L. 29

E

Emery, Janet L. 244
Engelmann, Shirley A. 87
Esenwein, Monica R. 92
Espinoza, Joe J. 248
Essary, Rhonda 125
Evelyn, Maureen M. 211

F

Farrell, Georgeanne 142
Farrington, Karla 169
Faustino, Cassandra 66
Feezor, Wilmetta 114
Fehl, Martha R. 17
Feldman, Kathi 206
Ferguson, Catherine 185
Fettig, Julia M. 150
Findley, Gary 83
Finney, Kimberly D. 198
Fleming, Ruby B. 30
Flickinger, Tom 50
Foglietta, Justin 203
Forde, Terry F. 116
Franklin, Veria 141
Fraser, Michelle M. 137
Furniss-Jones, Linda 300
Furstenberg, Pamela K. 79

G

Gajewska, Anna 197
Galeczka, Erika M. 233
Gary, Margie 78
George, Charlotte 160
Gerlach, Jill D. 225
Giauque, Keoni 35
Gibson, Lisa L. 222
Goddard, Sonya 261
Goodson, Annette 140
Gordon, Deborah 180
Gordon, Gene 257
Graham-Lemon, Cynthia 258
Granlund, Nancy L. 122
Gray, Peggi 91
Gray, Sharon L. 204
Green, India 213
Greenleaf, Nancy 9
Greenwood, Elizabeth A. 37
Gregory, Brenda Richmond 113
Grewal, Saachi 132
Grinstead, Andrea M. 154
Groh, Krista M. 115
Grygier, Barbara W. 96

H

Hadziomerovic, Mirela 298
Hallczuk, Franquie 274
Hamilton, Turner Wells 55
Harding, Marie 133
Harrell, Victoria 148
Hartsell, Amanda E. 273
Hattendorf, Cecilia 127
Hedstrom, Stephen W. 252
Hicks, Destiny C. 289
Hines, Vivienne 120
Hoard, Tiffany 62
Hochhalter, Marie 202
Hodges, Linda 256
Honea, Darlene 102

Honis, Ronald E. 130
Hooley, Kaitlyn 291
Horsnail, Alan 278
House, Dolores 105
Howard, Bobbie J. 164
Howell, Patti 229
Huntley, Gail 75
Hutchinson, Deb 3

I

Ison, Kellie 27

J

Jackson, Dana 201
Jackson, Wayne 1
Janotha, J. Emmi 317
Johnson, Anthony David 287
Johnson, Krisann 5
Jones-Walley, Georgette 95

K

Kelleher, Dan J. 82
Kelley, Barbara A. 21
Kelley, James E. 269
Kenney, Heidi 264
Kexcon, Tibor T. 226
King, Cynthia 103
King, Joy L. 224
Kinney, Denise S. 271
Kitts, Nancy F. 161
Kornfein, Gertrude 25
Kraus, Madison E. 294

L

Lamb, Stacy 267
Lankford, Leza 134
Larson, Daniel T. 171
Laurina, Mary 320
Lee, Alice K. 191
Lee, Donald C. 184
Lee, Frankie 268
Lee, Jae 69
Leis, Kyle 128
Lemons, Julee 235
Lessert, Renée 207
Lester, Linda Viviane 65
Levine, Bev 34
Lewis, Malinda S. 263
Link, Larry 209
Lloyd, Tanner 138
LoCicero, Karen M. 242
Loney, Sharon 106
Lory, Robert C. 126

M

MacEnulty, Elizabeth A. 296
Maddox, Alice 179
Madigan, Patricia M. 226
Magill, Kara L. 170
Martin, Robert D. 144
Mason, David R. 277
Mason-Davis, Velda 308
Massey, Marty 112
Matthews, Iris J. 31
Maxwell, Sheila 192
McClellen, Michael S. 230
McCready, Jordon L. 48
McGraw, Alice F. 311
McKinney, Mary Ann 188
Menking, Jean V. 124
Mercer, Joseph 51
Miller, Benjamin Joseph 300
Mimms, Tracy L. 97
Moffett, Kerry 93
Montoya, Lucy 109
Moore, Betty M. 64
Morgan, Easter D. 284
Mott, Fred T. 12
Moyer, Scott 49
Mueller, Maddi 302
Mulder, Arlene 153
Munson, Willis E. 168
Murray-Brault, Regina 8
Musto, Gregory M. 272
Mylod, Elizabeth 67

N

Nagyvathy, Emily Rose 310
Nance, Patricia 257
Neel, Saisa 260
Nguyen, Rosaleen K. 195
Nwosu, Margaret O. 157

O

Orsinger, Lorraine 223
Otwell, Katherine G. 147
Owens, Garry 186

P

Pagan, Jason 181
Pagliai, Ann T. 178
Parks, Judith R. 110
Peart, Terri-Karlene P. 312
Pelaez, Maria 270
Perez, Emily 165
Person, Jack 162
Pettigrew, Angie 14
Phyle, Lenore 234
Plymale, Laurie 236
Potenza, Elizabeth 167
Potts, James A. 277
Powell, Illene G. 210
Pratt, Hannah K. 285

R

Ravello, Amanda R. 280
Ray, Patricia K. 151
Redger, Taylor E. 246
Reece, Leila M. 43
Reese, Mary Ann Zumer 194
Rempe, Dave 19
Roberson, Tasha 166
Robertson, Marcella Gae 276
Robinson, Savalya 218
Rodgers, Rose 319
Rodriguez, Daphnie I. 303

Rodriguez, Drusila 76
Rogers, Kelly 318
Rogers, Rose M. 301
Romano, Beth A. 220
Ross, Carolyn J. 159
Rubio, Samaya O. 292
Russell, Betty J. 73

S

San Fillippo, Mary L. 149
Santiago, Luis R., Jr. 45
Scheel, Billie 187
Schmitt, Gloria E. 315
Schneider, Merylene R. 139
Schuchardt, David 111
Scott, Jerone 135
Seidel, Laura 255
Selvakumaran, Ashwini 58
Shaffer, Allen 19
Sharon, Sandra 121
Shay, Mary Anne 199
Sherman, John E. 237
Shook, Nelson N. 173
Shumate, Toni O'Kennon 208
Simini, Carol M. 212
Simpson, Donna G. 228
Sims-Aubrey, Minnie 86
Singh, Barbara 177
Sliko, Patti 163
Sloan, Judy 18
Smith, Jeannie C. 26
Smith, Judy Ann 253
Smith, Laura P. 68
Smith, Maxine A. 88
Snyder, Micayla 297
Solon, Rebecca S. 108
Sorrell, Alex 81
Sparks, Anna M. 172
Stearns, Mary E. 156
Swink-Jones, Alma L. 227
Szoo, Elsie M. 13

T

Tavangar, Zaul 53
Thomas, Mary M. 32
Torres, Melissa M. 219
Tower, Renee M. 36
Townsend, Beza 299
Trigili, Marjory 221
Tucker, Bonnie F. 60
Tucker, Gail M. 74

U

Ussery, Paige J. 150

V

Valnoha, Otto 44
Van Etten, Allen 189
Van Kleef, Tara 158
Van Ness, John 314
VanDeLoo, Joy Krista 251
Vatter, Marilyn S. 25
Vickers, Frances 49
Voss, Canaan M. 295

W

Walker, Ben 193
Walker, Jerome E. 63
Wall, Helen M. 99
Waltman, Gail 243
Walton, Gabrielle D. 119
Warholak, Mary 89
Warwick, James D. 28
Washington, Dominique Michelle 281
Welch, Dona D. 10
Wentz, JoAnne 104
Whelan, Carol 312
Wilcox, Keri L. 145
Wilhite, Kari 286
Willen, Nancy 175
Williams, Rick Rhythm 293
Williams, Wendi K. 94

Williamson, Margaret 107
Winston, Javon 98
Woitscheck, Jutta E. 217
Wood, Burnell Burns L. 262
Woods, Jana 249

Y

Yaccarino, Aida 183
Young, Lynda R. 196

Z

Zeibak, Juleigha M. 129